On the Field of Forensic Accounting
Skills and Abilities for Expert Witnesses

浅论法务会计领域专家证人的技能和能力

梁舒静 / 著

中国海洋大学出版社
·青岛·

图书在版编目（CIP）数据

浅论法务会计领域专家证人的技能和能力 / 梁舒静
著 . —青岛 : 中国海洋大学出版社 , 2019.4
ISBN 978-7-5670-2249-2

Ⅰ . ①浅… Ⅱ . ①梁… Ⅲ . ①司法会计学—研究
Ⅳ . ① D918.95

中国版本图书馆 CIP 数据核字（2019）第 114186 号

出版发行	中国海洋大学出版社		
社　　址	青岛市香港东路 23 号	**邮政编码**	266071
出 版 人	杨立敏		
网　　址	http://pub.ouc.edu.cn		
电子信箱	44066014 @qq.com		
订购电话	0532—85902573		
责任编辑	潘克菊	**电　　话**	0532—85902533
印　　制	日照报业印刷有限公司		
版　　次	2020 年 1 月第 1 版		
印　　次	2020 年 1 月第 1 次印刷		
成品尺寸	170mm×230mm		
印　　张	9		
字　　数	220 千		
印　　数	1~1000		
定　　价	36.00 元		

发现印装质量问题，请致电(0633)8221365,由印刷厂负责调换。

内容简介

本书旨在研究专家证人在法务会计领域的行为要求。在现有文献和各学者在此领域从事研究的基础上，通过对会计、专家证人和律师领域 79 名不同专业人员进行问卷调查，收集了初步数据。数据分析是借助各种统计、描述性统计和因子分析——主成分分析进行的。结果表明，丰富的工作经验、专业培训、高学历、良好的沟通技巧、怀疑态度和外交态度是法务会计领域专家证人取得成功的首要条件。其部分认为，法务会计师要想取得成功，还必须具备分析和调查技能。这项研究的未来迹象显示了一项更为详尽的研究，这项更为详尽的研究需要通过更大的样本和定性策略来分析数据。

Brief Introduction

This book seeks to investigate the requirements for an expert witness to act within the forensic accounting arena. Based on existing literature and studies conducted in this field by various scholars, the primary data were collected via questionnaire instrument administered on 79 different professionals from accountancy, expert witness and attorney field. Analysis of data was carried out with the help of various statistical, descriptive statistics and factor analysis - principal component analysis. The results show that extensive work experience, professional training, high academic qualifications, excellent communication skills, skepticism and diplomatic attitude are the foremost requirements to be successful for an expert witness within forensic accounting profession. It is also partially agreed that with analytical and investigative skills are required for forensic accountants to be successful. The futuristic implication of this study suggests a detailed research with larger sample and qualitative strategy for analysis of data.

目 录 Contents

第三章 / 研究方法
Chapter Ⅲ　Research Methodology

第四章 / 数据分析和结果
Chapter Ⅳ Data Analysis & Results

第五章 / 结论、局限和规范
Chapter V Conclusion Limitations & Implications

CHAPTER
I

第一章 / 引言

1.1 Introduction 导言

The purpose of this chapter is to familiarize the reader with the background of the research question followed by the main purpose, aims and objectives of the study. This chapter has three sections. The first section presents the experience of the study. It starts with a brief introduction to Forensic Accounting, followed by a description of the scope of forensic accounting and the role of Expert Witness. The following section outlines the research questions and motivation. The structure of this article is presented in the third section.

本章的目的是让读者熟悉研究问题的背景以及本研究的主要目的、目标和任务。本章分为三部分。第一部分介绍了研究的经验。它首先简要介绍了法务会计，然后介绍了法务会计的范围和专家证人的作用。接下来的第二部分简要概述了研究问题和动机。第三部分介绍了本书的结构。

1.2 Forensic Accounting 法务会计

Robert Montgomery, one of the co-founders of the American Accounting profession, once stated that the investigation of fraud is a most essential part of the auditor's duties in the corporate world, and there is nodebate that the auditor who is able to detect fraud is better than the auditor who cannot (Montgomery, 1916). In subsequent decades, however, conventional wisdom evolved to the point that auditors have refused primary responsibility for detecting frauds. Reported financial scandals like Barclays Bank interest rate manipulation, miss-selling of insurance (PPI) by banks in UK, WorldCom, Enron, Global Crossing, Qwest, Parmalat in USA etc. have continued to erode investor confidence in the capital market. Evidence from practitioners, regulatory authorities and the courts consistently suggests that a higher level of expertise is indispensable to analyze current complex financial transactions and events (Elmore, 2005). Consequently, this has generated opportunities for a new and specialized set of profession under accounting - Forensic Accounting.

美国会计职业的共同创始人之一罗伯特·蒙哥马利曾经说过，对舞弊的调查是审计师在企业界职责中最重要的一部分，有能力发现舞弊的审计师比没有能力发现舞弊的审计师更好，这一点是没有争议的（蒙哥马利，1916）。然而，在随后的几十年里，传统观念演变成审计师拒绝承担发现欺诈的责任。被报道的金融丑闻，如英国巴克莱银行操纵利率、世界通讯公司、安然、环球电讯、Qwest、美国帕尔马拉特等，不断打击着投资者对资本市场的信心。从业人员、监管当局和法院的证据一致表明，更高水平的专业知识对于分析当前复杂的金融交易和事件是必不可少的（Elmore，2005）。因此，这一切都为会计专业——法务会计——创造了新的专业机会。

Forensic Accounting is defined as the use of accurate data collection and analysis in the areas of litigation support consulting, expert witnessing, and fraud examination (Elmore, 2005). It applies accounting, statistics, research, economic concepts and techniques to legal problems or prospective legal problems (Singleton & Singleton, 2010). Okoye & Akamobi (2009) defines "Forensic Accounting is the combination of utilizing accounting, auditing and investigative skills to advance in legal matters. It is the science that ideals with the relevance and practice of economic, accounting, tax and auditing expertise to analyze, investigate, inquire, study and investigate matters in criminal law". Therefore, many people make use words like forensic accounting, fraud auditing and fraud investigation interchangeably but there is differentiation amongst these three terminologies. According to Singleton & Singleton (2010), the difference is related to one's goals. Financial auditor enables a person to furnish an opinion as to whether a series of transactions is presented fairly according to GAAP and besides his work is related to deal with financial statements; Fraud auditing is a specialized instruction which investigates a particular form of criminal activities and reviews financial statements and documentation for the purposes of investigation; while Forensic Accounting is a general term used to describe any financial analysis that may result in legal consequences (Singleton & Singleton,

2010）. The materiality level of Forensic Accounting is much more broader and wider than that of normal financial auditing and fraud investigation（Singleton & Singleton, 2010）. Forensic accountants utilize their extensive knowledge of economics, financial reporting techniques, accounting and auditing standards and procedures, data management and analysis techniques for investigating and revealing frauds and scandals and other litigation procedures to present their duties（Singleton & Singleton, 2010）. Therefore, forensic accountant's responsibilities include （Okoye & Akamobi, 2009）:

　　法务会计的定义是指在诉讼支持咨询、专家见证和欺诈检查领域使用准确的数据进行收集和分析（Elmore，2005 年）。它将会计、统计、研究、经济概念和技术应用于法务会计用于解决诉讼中遇到的和将面临的财务会计问题（Singleton & Singleton，2010）。Okoye 和 Akamobi（2009）将其定义为"法务会计是利用会计、审计和调查技能在法律事务上取得进展的结合。它是一门科学，能够运用经济、会计、税务和审计专业的知识来分析、调查、询问、研究和调查刑法问题的相关性和实践性"。因此，很多人交替使用法务会计、舞弊审计和舞弊调查等词语，但这三个术语有所区别。根据 Singleton & Singleton（2010）的说法，这种差异与个人的目标有关。财务审计师使一个人能够就一系列交易是否按照一般公认会计原则（GAAP）以及他的工作是否与处理财务报表有关提出意见。欺诈审计舞弊审计是一项专门的指示，它调查特定形式的犯罪活动，并为调查目的审查财务报表和文件。而法务会计是一个通用术语，用于描述可能导致法律后果的任何财务分析（Singleton & Singleton，2010）。法务会计的重要性水平比一般财务审计和舞弊调查的重要性水平更广泛（Singleton & Singleton，2010）。法务会计师利用其广泛的经济学知识、财务报告技术、会计和审计准则和程序、调查和揭露欺诈和丑闻的数据管理和分析技术以及其他诉讼程序来履行职责（Singleton & Singleton，2010）。因此，法务会计师的职责包括（Okoye & Akamobi, 2009）:

• Scrutinizing and examining financial evidence;

审查和检查财务证据

• Developing electronic reports in order to analyse and present of financial evidence for legal matters;

编制电子报告以便分析和提交法律事项的财务证据

• Communicating their findings in the form of reports and if necessary;

必要时以报告的形式传达调查结果

• Assisting in legal proceedings, including testifying in court as an expert witness and preparing visual aids to support trial evidence.（MLA）

协助法律诉讼，包括作为专家证人在法庭上作证和准备视觉辅助工具以支持审判证据。（MLA）

1.3 Scope of Forensic Accounting 法务会计的范围

Earlier, it was believed that detection and prevention of frauds, scandals or office crimes were part of normal accounting functions. But the knowledge of Forensic Accounting has changed this view by emphasizing that the auditor is just a monitor but not an investigator or a preventer. They only stay for the compliance of a company's books to GAAPs, auditing standards and company policies（Singleton & Singleton, 2010）. Hence, there is a need for an equivalent of "Bloodhound" in accounting to sniff out frauds.A forensic accountant is to sniff out frauds, criminal transactions out of the financial records of corporate entities, banks or any other organizations（Crumbley, Heitger & Smith, 2011）. Therefore, according to Crumbley, Heitger & Smith（2011）, a forensic accountant is a financial detective with a suspicious mind who can pull out the latent truth with the help of the knowledge base of accounting, law and criminology with investigative auditing skills and assist in dispute resolution（see Figure 1）.

早些时候，人们认为发现预防欺诈、丑闻或办公室犯罪是正常会计职能的一部分。但法务会计的知识改变了这种看法，强调审计师只是一个监测者，而不是调查者或预防者。它们只是为了公司账簿符合公认会计准则、审计标准和公司政策（Singleton & Singleton，2010）。因此，在会计上需要相当于"猎犬"的手段来查出欺诈行为。法务会计师将从公司实体、银行或任何其他组织的财务记录中查出欺诈、犯罪交易（Crumbley, Heitger & Smith, 2011）。因此，根据 Crumbley, Heitger 和 Smith（2011）的说法，法务会计师是一个有可疑头脑的金融侦探，他可以借助会计、法律和犯罪学的知识基础，运用调查审计技巧来揭露隐藏的真相并帮助解决纠纷问题（见图1）。

Forensic Accountant 法务会计师

Figure 1　Scope of Forensic Accounting（Crumbley, Heitger & Smith, 2011）

图 1　法务会计的范围（Crumbley, Heitger & Smith, 2011）

The increased business complexities in this cut throat competition era have enhanced the demand for forensic accounting discipline. According to Singleton & Singleton（2010）, forensic accounting could be applied to following general areas:

在这个竞争激烈的时代，日益增加的业务复杂性增强了人们对法务会计学科的需求。根据 Singleton & Singleton（2010），法务会计可以应用于以下普遍领域：

• Litigation Support - It represents accurate presentation of financial issues encompassing existing litigation. If the dispute reaches the courtroom, he / she may testify as an expert witness（Pagano & Buckhoff, 2005）. This would be discussed in detail in the later part of the research.

诉讼支持——此领域准确地介绍了包括现有诉讼在内的财务问题。如果纠纷诉诸法院解决，他 / 她可以作为专家证人作证（Pagano & Buckhoff, 2005）。这一部分将在后面的研究中详细讨论。

• Corporate Investigation - In this, forensic accountants use their auditing and investigative skills to analyze events that have already occurred and to develop assumptions about what might have happened and describe them in reports. They also aid in allegations ranging from kickbacks and unfair dismissals to internal situations involving allegations of management or employee malfeasance.

公司调查——在这方面，法务会计师利用他们的审计和调查技能来分析已经发生的事件，对可能发生的事情提出假设并在报告中加以描述。他们也会协助指控，这些指控从收取回扣和不公平解雇到关于管理和员工渎职的多种内部情况。

• Criminal Matters - Forensic Accountants can also put their efforts together and prevent white-collar crimes like scandals, vendor frauds, customer frauds, and stock market manipulations. Also, they could act as expert witness in judicial courts while giving testimony.

刑事事项——法务会计师还可以齐心协力，防止丑闻、供应商欺诈、客户欺诈和股票市场操纵等白领犯罪。此外，他们还可以在司法法庭作证时充当专家证人。

• Insurance Claims – Forensic Accountants can also assist with preparation of and valuation of insurance claims on behalf of insured and insurers to assess the integrity and quantum of the claim. Certain insurance claims may require historical analysis and other accounting measures to assess the claim.

保险索赔——法务会计师还可以代表被保险人和保险人协助准备和评估保险索赔以评估索赔的完整性和数量。某些保险索赔可能需要历史分析和其他会计措施来评估索赔。

• Government Regulations/ Compliance – Forensic Accountants can assist entities to achieve regulatory compliance by following appropriate legislation, law or contract terms.

政府法规 / 合规性——法务会计师可以通过遵循适当的立法、法律或合同条款，协助实体实现法规合法性。

Crumbley, Heitger & Smith（2011）and other scholars have discretely identified more areas like stakeholders and ownership disputes, matrimonial dispute cases; dispute settlements, where forensic accounting is widely used to assess claims or investigate them in detail.

Crumbley, Heitger & Smith（2011）等学者已经确定了在更多的领域，如利益相关者和所有权纠纷、婚姻纠纷案件，纠纷解决，法务会计被广泛用于评估索赔或对索赔进行详细调查。

1.4 An Expert Witness 专家证人

One of the most important reforms in the context of expert witness was that of Woolf reform which was incorporated into the civil practices in England and Scotland and defined a distinction between Expert witness and a professional witness（Casey, 2003）. The main objectives of Woolf reforms were to reduce cost, speed up lengthy trials and to codify the role of an expert witness（Rix, 2000）. During a legal proceeding if the opposing party is found at guilt in investigation, then this may lead to either legal action（judicial court case）or out of court settlement. The forensic accountant must understand the legal process because in case of legal action, there would be a compulsory requirement of an outside expert to give testimony, which is commonly referred as an Expert Witness（Telpner & Mostek, 2002）. The person who knows or understands the details, allegations and matters about which testimony is going to take place in the court room, and the person possess special knowledge, skills, training or experience related to testimony is called as an Expert Witness（Pagano & Buckhoff, 2005）. Therefore, an expert witness should be the person who holds technical, scientific or other specialized knowledge that will assist the trier of fact in understanding the evidence or determining a fact in issue（Scarrow, 2002）.

专家证人方面最重要的改革之一是伍尔夫改革，这一改革被纳入英格兰和苏格兰的民事事件并界定了专家证人和专业证人之间的区别（Casey, 2003）。伍尔夫改革的主要目标是降低成本、加快冗长的审判和编纂专家证人的角色（Rix, 2000）。在法律诉讼过程中，如果对方在调查中被判有罪，那么这可能导致法律诉讼（司法案件）或庭外和解。法务会计必须了解法律程序，因为在法律诉讼中，是强制要求外部专家进行作证的，这些外部专家通常被称为专家证人（Telpner & Mostek, 2002）。知道或理解在法庭上将要进行的证词的细节、指控和事项并具有与证词有关的专门知识、技能、培训或经验的人被称为专家证人（Pagano & Buckhoff, 2005）。因此，专家证人应是掌握技术、科学或其他专门知识的人，这些知识将有助于事实调查者理解证据或确定有争议的事实（Scarrow, 2002）。

The role of expert witness, as suggested above, is to represent the testimony in the courtroom. Now, the judge at the court will decide whether the person should be skilled and eligible enough to be an expert witness or not（Telpner & Mostek, 2002）. If those people are qualified, they will be allowed to provide or give expert testimony. To determine whether a witness is qualified, the judge must be convinced whether a person knows or understands all matters pertaining to testimony that is going to be held in courtroom（Telpner & Mostek, 2002）. The expert witness's qualification is then presented to attorney, where opposing attorney will have rights to challenge the expert witness's qualifications by asking him or her relevant questions to testimony（Telpner & Mostek, 2002）. The opposing attorney's main goal is to diminish the jury's or judge's confidence in expert witness opinion. If a person is qualified enough to counteract and understand the matters related to testimony, then he / she will be smart enough to handle those objections from opposing attorney（Pagano & Buckhoff, 2005）. Expert Witness will be judged on their view that has been formed based on the facts presumed by the expert and on the facts that have been presented by others. Again, formulation of this opinion is dependent on the knowledge or skills of the expert witness, and how they produce and deduce the information available. This quality in expert witness distinguishes themselves from non-experts in courtroom （Telpner & Mostek, 2002）.

如上所述，专家证人的作用是在法庭上陈述证词。现在，法庭的法官将决定该人是否有足够的技能和资格成为专家证人（Telpner & Mostek，2002）。如果这些人有资格，他们将被允许提供专家证词。为了确定证人是否合格，必须使法官确信一个人是否知道或理解与将要在法庭上庭审的所有事项（Telpner & Mostek，2002）。专家证人的资格随后被提交给律师，在律师处，对立的律师有权通过询问专家证人的相关证词来质疑专家证人的资格（Telpner & Mostek，2002）。对方律师的主要目的是降低陪审团或法官对专家证人意见的信心。如果一个人有资格反驳和理解与证词有关的问题，那么他 / 她将足够聪明地处理来自对方律师的反对意见（Pagano &Buckhoff, 2005）。根据专家推定的事实和其他人提出的事实形成的意见，专家证人才被得以评判。同样，这一意见的形成取决于专家证人的知识或技能以及他们如何产生和推断可用的信息。专家证人的这种素质与法庭上的非专家的素质是不同的（Telpner & Mostek，2002）。

Generally, Expert Witnesses are the only ones who are permitted to provide their opinions in court（Scarrow, 2002）. Non-expert witnesses must enclose testimony to that which they have perceived or to mind that is not based on any kind of specialized knowledge（Scarrow, 2002）. This would include opinions related to case. In the course of providing the court with their opinions expert witnesses are asked to do for things separately（Scarrow, 2002）:

一般来说，只有专家证人才被允许在法庭上发表意见（Scarrow，2002）。

非专家证人必须附上证词，证明他们所看到或想到的不是基于任何专门知识的证词（Scarrow，2002）。这包括与案件有关的意见。在向法庭提供意见的过程中，专家证人被要求单独处理事情（Scarrow，2002）：

· Establish the facts;

确定事实；

· Interpret the facts;

解释事实；

· Define the quality of care and evaluate the control exercised in the case against that standard;

确定审慎思考的质量并评估在违反该标准的情况下实施的控制；

· Comment on the opposing counsel's facts and opinions.

评论对方律师的事实和意见。

Based on their expert knowledge, expert witnesses produce their opinions in the courtroom and try to persuade jury or judge in favor of their facts and figures produced. But in corporate investigations and scandals in companies, an expert witness could be a corporate forensic accountant as well （Crumbley, Heitger & Smith, 2011）. Forensic accountants play an extensive and proactive role in fraud risk reduction by designing and performing extended procedures, being a part of the statutory audit, acting as an adviser to audit committees, a fraud deterrence engagement, and assisting in investment analyst research. These skills and expertise could not be obtained purely by getting educated in a particular area but also come with relevant experience & skills, interest, personality and intelligence.

专家证人根据自己的专业知识在法庭上发表自己的意见，试图说服陪审团或法官支持他们提出的事实和数字。但在公司调查和公司丑闻中，专家证人也可以是公司法务会计师（Crumbley, Heitger & Smith, 2011）。法务会计师通过设计和执行扩展程序，作为法定审计的一部分充当审计委员会的顾问、阻止欺诈的参与以及协助投资分析师研究从而在减少欺诈风险方面发挥了广泛和积极的作用。这些技能和专门知识不能仅仅通过在特定领域接受教育来获得，还需要相关的经验和技能、兴趣、个性和智力才能获得。

1.5 Aims and Objectives 目标和任务

Financial scandals and frauds are non-violent and in most of the cases are committed by people, who are delegated with the responsibility of taking care of funds or their collaborators. This is because people, who should have this first-hand information, are those who can easily manipulate or commit these crimes. Therefore, this has resulted in great demand for the services rendered by the forensic accountants. They provide their services were the employee indulges in illegal activities or where the employees are caught to have committed fraud. The job of a forensic accountant is to assess and investigate the fraud committed in the organization and to settle disputes. The dispute could be settled down out of court or inside the courtroom. In order to represent the testimony in courtroom, there has to be Expert Witness to defy it. Therefore, this book aims to address the following research questions:

财务丑闻和欺诈都是非暴力的，而且在大多数情况下，都是由负责管理资金或其合作者的人所为。这是因为掌握这第一手资料的人，是可以轻易操纵犯下这些罪行的人的。因此，对法务会计师的服务需求很大。如果员工沉迷于非法活动或被发现有欺诈行为，他们会为此提供服务。法务会计师的工作是评估和调查组织内的欺诈行为并解决纠纷，纠纷可以在庭外或法庭内解决。为了在法庭上陈述证词，那么就必须有专家证人来反驳。因此，本书旨在解决以下研究问题：

"What should be the requirements for an expert witness to be sufficiently independent within the forensic accounting？"

"专家证人在法务会计中充分独立的要求是什么？"

Crumbley, Heitger & Smith（2011）mentions the importance of forensic accountant, but extremely little research has been carried out in this area. This research focuses on specific skills, competencies, characteristics of a forensic accountant, which can be used in demonstration while presenting themselves in the courtroom as an expert witness. The main purpose of this research is to investigate the importance and relevance of forensic accounting in a financial period for expert witnessing nowadays. This research examines the role of expert witness within forensic accounting from the perspectives of scholars and practitioners. Furthermore, it answers questions as follows:

Crumbley，Heitger 和 Smith 提到了法务会计的重要性，但在这方面的研究非常少。本研究的重点是法务会计的具体技能、能力和特点，可以在法庭上作为专家证人进行演示。本研究的主要目的是探讨财务期间法务会计在当今专家见证中的重要性和相关性。本研究从学者和实务人员的角度考察了专家证人在法务会计中的作用。此外，它还回答了以下问题：

· What are the main requirements to become a successful expert witness ?

成为成功的专家证人的主要要求是什么？

· Do they require any skills, or specialized knowledge apart from material testimony ?

除了物证之外，他们是否需要任何技能或专门知识？

· How is this knowledge gained ?

这种知识是如何获得的？

· How can an expert witness face the challenges of an opposing party in court during testimony ?

专家证人在作证时如何面对对方的挑战？

· Can forensic accountant be an expert witness ?

法务会计师能成为专家证人吗？

The main objective of this book is to examine the existing literature on forensic accounting and establish the role of an expert witness within forensic accounting. Furthermore, it also examines skills, knowledge and characteristics of a forensic accountant and expert witness respectively. Thereafter, they are linked to each other and are administered through questionnaires in order to test them in a specific set of non-random sample. To achieve the objective, two stages will be applied. Firstly existing literature will be reviewed for the preliminary study of forensic accounting and expert testimony. Secondly, a number of the self-administered questionnaire will be used. The initial research will be compared to the experiences in a specific set of a random sample of relevant people in the field. The purpose of this stage is to provide clearer and empirically grounded skills, knowledge and characteristics required for an expert testimony to be sufficiently independent within the forensic accounting.

本书的主要目的是考察现有的法务会计文献，确立专家证人在法务会计中的作用。此外，它还考察了法务会计和专家证人各自的技能、知识和特点。此后，它们相互联系并通过问卷进行管理以便在一组特定的非随机样本中进行测试。为实现这一目标，将会分其两个阶段进行。首先将对现有文献进行综述，以便对法务会计和专家证词进行初步研究。其次，将使用一些自行填写的问卷而且最初的研究将与特定的一组随机抽样的相关人员的经验进行比较。这一阶段的目的是提供专家证词在法务会计中充分独立所需的更清晰和有经验基础的技能、知识和特征。

1.6 Dissertation Structure 论文结构

This dissertation is comprised of five chapters. It starts with an introduction, followed by literature review of relevant studies, research methodology, data analysis and concluding remarks.

本文共分五章。首先是引言，然后是相关研究文献综述、研究方法论述、数据分析和结束语。

Chapter Ⅰ : Introduction
第一章：引言

This chapter introduces the background of this research followed by first purpose, aims and objectives for carrying out such a study. The background of study is provided with an introduction to Forensic Accounting, its scope in today's era and role of expert witness. It is followed by aims and objectives of the study and concluded by providing an overall structure of this dissertation.

本章首先介绍了本研究的背景，然后介绍了本研究的目的、目标和任务。本文的研究背景是介绍法务会计及其在当今时代的范围和专家证人的作用。接下来是研究的目的和任务，最后给出了本文的总体结构。

Chapter Ⅱ : Literature Review
第二章：文献综述

This chapter covers the discussion of skill set required to be a forensic accountant and expert witness. Furthermore, it attempts to explain different competencies, skills, required characteristics and knowledge level mentioned by different scholars like Singleton & Singleton(2010), Telpner & Mostek (2002), Scarrow (2002) etc. to be a forensic accountant and expert witness in testimony. All this discussion is linked to each other, to further understand the requirements for an expert witness to be sufficiently independent within the forensic accounting field. Therefore, the chapter is fundamentally broken down into five main parts. The first part focuses on small introduction to forensic accountants and how they differ from other traditional accountants. The second part introduces the skills, knowledge, competencies and characteristics required on forensic accountant to perform his duties. The third part provides a brief introduction to expert witness and moves to skills, competencies and characteristics required by an Expert Witness in the courtroom to defy the testimony. The fourth part will discuss relevant literature studies relating expert witness and forensic accounting with each other. Finally, it deduces hypotheses that need to be tested in order to explore requirements for an expert witness to be sufficiently independent within forensic accounting. In general, this chapter provides the basis for the next stage by endeavoring to combine all the research done in this area by scholars.

本章讨论作为法务会计和专家证人所需的技能。此外，它试图解释不同学者如 Singleton & Singleton（2010）、Telpner &Mostek（2002）、Scarrow（2002）等所提到的作为法务会计和鉴定人的不同能力、技能、要求的特征和知识水平。所有这些讨论都是相互关联的，目的是进一步了解专家证人在法务会计领域中充分独立的要求。因此，本章从根本上分为五个主要部分。第一部分重点介绍了法务会计的一些基本概念以及法务会计与其他传统会计的区别。第二部分介绍了法务会计人员履行职责所需的技能、知识、能力和特点。第三部分简要介绍了专家证人，并介绍了专家证人在法庭上挑衅证言所需要的技能、能力和特点。第四部分是专家证人与法务会计的相关文献研究。最后，它推导出需要检验的假设用以探索专家证人在法务会计中充分独立的要求。总体而言，这一章通过努力将学者们在这一领域的研究成果结合起来并为下一阶段的工作提供了基础。

Chapter Ⅲ : Research Methodology
第三章：研究方法

This chapter aims to explain the method applied to gather data and develop hypotheses. It will also explain why a deductive method with positivist epistemology will be used and the self-administered will be followed by questionnaires quantitative approach. In addition, it demonstrates how basic data via questionnaires and secondary data via literature review, journals and books is collected. It is concluded with ethical issues; a sampling process; how reliability and validity are managed; it will also mention the limitations to the approach.

本章旨在解释用于收集数据和提出假设的方法。它还将解释为什么将使用实证认识论的演绎方法和自我管理式的问卷定量方法。此外，本章还阐述了如何通过问卷调查和文献综述、期刊和书籍等方式收集基础数据和二手数据。最后通过伦理问题，抽样过程和如何管理信度和效度等得出结论。同时本章还提到这种方法的局限性。

Chapter Ⅳ : Data Analysis and Discussion
第四章：数据分析和结果

This chapter analyses the information achieved via self-administered questionnaires. Charts and tables are used in this chapter to clearly present the frequency distributions of respondents. Furthermore, different statistics methods, such as, factor analysis and related techniques to test hypotheses are used. They are deduced in the literature review of this dissertation. Finally, a discussion of the results against the existing literatures held following completion of the entire chapter.

本章所分析的数据信息是通过自我管理问卷所获得的信息。本章使用图表清楚地展示了受访者的频率分布。此外，还采用了不同的统计方法，如因子分析和相关技术来检验假设。它们是通过本文的文献综述中推导出来的。最后，本章对全文完成的结果与现有文献情况进行了讨论。

Chapter Ⅴ : Conclusions，Limitation，and Implications
第五章：结论、局限和规范

In this chapter, the key issues and analysis of this research will be summarized. The academic and real-world practical contributions are also discussed in this chapter. Thereafter, it underlines recommendations for future research to be carried out in this field. Finally, bibliography has a list of references and Appendix A displays the copy of the self-administered questionnaire.

本章将对本研究的关键问题和分析进行总结，还讨论了学术界和现实世界的实际贡献。随后强调了今后在这一领域开展研究的建议。最后，参考书目有一个参考书目列表，而附录 A 是自填问卷的副本。

CHAPTER
II

LITERATURE
REVIEW

第二章 / 文献综述

2.1 Introduction 导言

Although forensic accountants utilize their extensive knowledge of economics, financial reporting techniques, accounting and auditing standards and procedures, data management and analysis techniques for investigating and revealing frauds and scandals, but the important area of concern in this field is to study their characteristics, skills or specialized which makes them special to carry out these tasks in the corporate world. Furthermore, the main aim of this research is to identify which of them makes to carry out and perform tasks of expert witness in a testimony in the courtroom. This will help us to find special characteristics required for an expert witness to be sufficiently independent within the forensic accounting. This chapter reviews the existing literature studies characteristics, competencies, knowledge and skills present in forensic accountant and expert witness. The aim of this research is to understand and explore the requirements for an expert witness to be sufficiently independent within the forensic accounting. An important not is that this study will use the works skills and abilities interchangeably referring to an individual's expertise. Also the word personality trait refers to an individual's distinguished quality.

尽管法务会计师利用其广泛的经济学知识、财务报告技术、会计和审计准则和程序、数据管理和分析技术来调查和揭露欺诈和丑闻，但这一领域的重要关注区域是研究他们的特点、技能或专门知识，使他们能够在企业界执行这些任务来显得特殊。此外，本研究的主要目的是确定哪些因素可以使专家证人从事和执行作证的任务。这将有助于我们找到专家证人在法务会计中充分独立所需的特殊特性。本章回顾了法务会计和专家证人的现有文献研究特点、能力、知识和技能。本研究的目的是了解和探讨专家证人在法务会计中充分独立的要求。重要的不是这项研究将会交替使用特指个人专长的工作技能和能力。人格特质一词也指个人的杰出品质。

2.2 Forensic Accountants 法务会计师

A Forensic Accountant is an individual who assists organizations and individuals mainly to provide support in the use of his outstanding reviews for fraud detection, litigation support, criminal matters, and especially through expert witness testimony (Harris & Brown, 2000) . Forensic accountants employ their individual ability to the collection of various assignments and are usually appointed to determine whether there has been any intentional misrepresentation associated with a company's financial records (DiGabriele, 2008) . Fraudulent misrepresentation can range from overvaluation of inventory and improper capitalization of expenses to misstatement of earnings and embezzlement (Harris & Brown, 2000; Messmer, 2004) . Large conglomerates often employ forensic accountants for regulating and evaluating potential business transactions (DiGabriele, 2008) . They help organizations to assess an organization's net worth while making important decisions like mergers, acquisitions, buy out or sell out its subsidiaries etc. and ensure that a buyer is well-informed about the target company's financial position and cost while looking for signs of suspicious accounting activity (Harris & Brown, 2000) . Forensic accountants also provide accounting expertise during existing or pending litigation (DiGabriele, 2008) . It is primarily focused on computing compensations in cases of personal injuries, product liability, contract disputes and uncovering hidden assets in complex cases (DiGabriele, 2008) . These types of services may culminate in the forensic accountant's providing expert witness testimony (Durtschi, 2003; Messmer, 2004; Peterson & Reider, 2001; Ramaswamy, 2005) . Therefore, it is clear that to be a forensic accountant, a person requires knowledge, skills and competencies to a greater degree as summarized by Okoye and Akamobi (2009) . Okoye and Akamobi (2009) point out that a forensic accountant distinguishes himself from financial accountant in following ways:

法务会计师是协助组织和个人的独立个体，主要是为利用其出色的审查手段对欺诈侦查、诉讼支持、刑事事项，特别是通过专家证人证词来提供支持（Harris & Brown，2000）。法务会计师利用自己的个人能力来收集各种任务，通常被任命来确定是否存在与公司财务记录相关的故意失实陈述（DiGabriele，2008）。欺诈性虚假陈述可从库存高估和支出资本化不当造成的收入和贪污错报（Harris & Brown，2000；Messmer，2004）。大型企业集团经常雇用法务会计师来监管和评估潜在的商业交易（DiGabriele，2008）。他们帮助组织评估组织的净值，同时做出类似兼并、收购、买断或出售子公司等重要决定，并确保买方在寻找可疑会计活动的迹象时，充分了解目标公司的财务状况和成本（Harris & Brown，2000）。法务会计师还在现有诉讼或未决诉讼中提供会计专门知识（DiGabriele，2008）。主要侧重于人身伤害、产品责任、合同纠纷、隐匿资产等复杂案件中的计算补偿问题（DiGabriele，2008）。这些类型的服务可能最终导致法务会计师提供专家证人证言（Durtschi，2003；Messmer，2004；Peterson & Reider，2001；Ramaswamy，2005）。因此，很显然如 Okoye 和 Akamobi（2009）所概述的那样，作为一名法务会计师更需要知识、技能和能力。Okoye 和 Akamobi（2009）指出，法务会计师通过以下方式将自己与财务会计区分开来：

· It requires a greater degree of professional skepticism. A forensic accountant is not required to accept explanations and documents at face value.

这需要更大程度的专业怀疑精神。法务会计不需要接受表面价值上的解释和文件。

· They dig out facts and figures much deeper than a traditional accountant who just works on face value.

他们挖掘的事实和数字要比传统会计更深，后者只是按表面价值工作。

· A forensic accountant is more familiar with the malpractices of employees and stakeholders regarding how they can abuse or misuse the system and commit frauds, scandals than any other traditional accountant.

法务会计师更熟悉员工和利益相关者对于如何滥用或滥用系统以及犯欺诈丑闻等弊端的做法，而不同于任何其他传统会计师。

· They are more experienced in collecting facts and figures. They know when and where to look for exact evidence and how to extract and use the data for litigation services.

他们在收集事实和数字方面有更多经验。他们知道何时何地寻找确切的证据以及如何提取和使用这些数据来进行诉讼服务。

· They are more adept at interviewing company's personal, witness and subjects.

他们更擅长与公司的员工、证人和问题的面谈。

Since, all professional accountants work within the business and legal framework, they all are in a sense, forensic accountants. But, it is the level of engagement, knowledge, skills and competencies in their area distinguishes forensic accountants from other traditional accountants.

因为，所有的专业会计师都是在商业和法律框架内工作的，从某种意义上说，他们都是法务会计师。但是，法务会计师与其他传统会计师的区别在于他们所在领域的参与程度、知识、技能和能力。

2.3 Skills and Competencies of Forensic Accountants
法务会计师的技能和能力

Forensic accounting is the act of recognizing, recording, obtaining, organizing and verifying past financial figures or other accounting activities for resolving current or prospective legal disputes or using such recent financial information for analyzing future economic information to resolve legal disputes (Crumbley, Heitger & Smith, 2011). Therefore, a forensic accountant has to focus on the past, although it may do so in order to look forward, perform for a specific legal forum or in anticipation of presentation before a legal forum or may be proactively appointed in a wide variety of risk management assignments within a corporate environment as a matter of right, without the necessity of allegations (Crumbley, Heitger & Smith, 2011). In order to perform their duties, they need to have specialized skills, knowledge, competences and characteristics in order to perform their duties and should have a strong understanding of their subject. This report will focus on all of them in a subsequent section.

法务会计是指确认、记录、获取、组织和核实过去的财务数字或其他会计活动，以解决当前或未来的法律纠纷或利用这些最近的财务信息分析未来的经济信息以解决法律纠纷的行为（Crumbley, Heitger & Smith, 2011）。因此，法务会计师必须着眼于过去，尽管这样做可能是为了向前看，为特定的法律论坛履行职责，或者期待在法律论坛上陈述，或者可以在公司环境中的各种风险管理任务中积极主动地被任命为合适人选，而不需要被任命（Crumbley, Heitger & Smith, 2011）。要履行职责，需要有专门的技能、知识、能力和特点才能履行职责，并对自己的学科有很强的理解。本报告将在随后的一节中重点讨论这些所有的问题。

2.3.1 Required Skills of Forensic Accountants
法务会计师必备技能

According to Singleton & Singleton（2010）, there should be several mandatory skills, knowledge and abilities which forensic accountants must. These skills can be gained with a combination of education and experience. They are as follows:

根据 Singleton & Singleton（2010）的说法，法务会计师必须具备几项必备的技能、知识和能力。这些技能可以通过教育和经验相结合来获得。它们分别如下：

· **Ability to understand frauds with minimal information**–As fraud investigation always start with minimum or scarce amount of information, the forensic accountant should have the ability to judge the possible plot and the possible manner in which it was been committed. This is also termed as "Fraud theory approach"（Singleton & Singleton, 2010）.

用最少的信息理解欺诈的能力—由于欺诈调查总是从最少或稀少的信

息量开始，因此法务会计师应该具备判断可能的阴谋和其可能的实施方式的能力。这也被称为"欺诈理论方法"（Singleton & Singleton，2010）。

· **Interviewing skills** ‑ As through out the course of seeking and collecting information and evidences about the fraud, the forensic accountant should be able to identify the target audience to be interviewed. Another important aspect of this skill is to handle the confessions in such a way that it could be admissable in court of law. This was also mentioned in a study conducted by Messmer（2004）.

面试技巧——在寻找和收集有关欺诈的信息和证据的过程中，法务会计师应该能够识别要面试的目标群众。这一技巧的另一个重要方面是以法庭可以接受的方式处理供词。Messmer（2004）进行的一项研究也提到了这一点。

· **Mind‑set** ‑ The forensic accountant should have skeptic behaviour and mind set towards people. He should never fully trust people, nor he should fully distrust people. This is because financial statements and audit methodologies are never designed to detect fraud, but rather they are designed to identify financial misstatements. Therefore in order to investigate frauds, logic, problem‑solving and detective skills are of paramount success for them（AICPA, 2008）

心态——法务会计师应对人的行为和心态持怀疑态度。他不应该完全信任人也不应该完全不信任人。这是因为财务报表和审计方法从来不是为了发现欺诈，而是为了识别财务错报。因此，为了调查欺诈，逻辑、解决问题和侦查技巧对他们来说是成功至关重要的因素（AICPA，2008）。

· **Knowledge of evidence** ‑ The forensic accountant must fully understand the signs which he / she has found out during inspection. How it to be found, how investigation was conducted from beginning until end etc. This is because evidence should not be considered as inadmissible in front of judicial court of law （Singleton & Singleton, 2010）.

证据知识——法务会计师必须完全理解他/她在检查过程中发现的迹象。如何发现，如何从头到尾进行调查等。这是因为在司法法庭面前，证据不应被视为不可受理（Singleton &Singleton，2010）。

·**Presentation of findings** - The forensic accountant must have excellent communication and presentation skills in order to present the evidence before the judicial court of law. This presentation could be oral or written or demonstrative aids depending on its nature（Singleton & Singleton, 2010; Messmer, 2004）.

陈述调查结果——法务会计师必须具有出色的沟通和陈述技能以便向司法法庭陈述证据。这种介绍是口头的、书面的还是演示性的取决于它的性质（Singleton & Singleton，2010；Messmer，2004）。

·**Knowledge of investigative techniques** - The forensic accountant should be able to acquire further information, documents and related evidence once the fraud has been identified. It is also imperative for them to know intricacies of GAAP, financial statement disclosure and systems of internal control wherever applicable in order to investigate fraud further（Rasmussen & Leauanae, 2004; Harris & Brown, 2000）.

调查技术知识——一旦发现欺诈行为，法务会计师应能够获得更多信息、文件和相关证据。为了进一步调查欺诈行为，他们还必须尽可能了解一般公认会计原则、财务报表披露和内部控制制度的复杂性（Rasmussen & Leauanae, 2004; Harris & Brown, 2000）。

·**Investigative skills and mentality** - These are required while presenting testimony in front of court of law. This is to ensure other party the benefit of doubt that proper interpretations is giving to all transactions while investigating fraud. It is also required by litigation support to ensure that proper calculations of lost profit has been applied.（Singleton & Singleton, 2010; DiGabriele, 2008）

调查技能和心态——在法庭面前作证时需要这些技能和心态。这是为了确保另一方在调查欺诈的同时，对所有交易做出正确的解释。诉讼支持也要求确保正确计算利润损失。（Singleton & Singleton, 2010; DiGabriele, 2008）

·**Identification of financial issues** - When forensic accountants are assigned to task where there are rumors, complaints and allegations, it is important for them to know and identify the significant financial issues and repercussions of claim. (Singleton & Singleton, 2010)

财务问题的识别——当法务会计师被指派承担有谣言、投诉和指控的任务时，他们必须了解并识别重大财务问题和索赔的影响。(Singleton & Singleton, 2010)

· **Interpretation of financial information** – This is one of the most important skills all accountants should have it. It is very uncommon for any transaction or series of events to have only one explanation. Therefore, in case of investigations, the forensic accountants must able to identify and interpret all financial information related to investigation of fraud committed. (Singleton & Singleton, 2010; Harris & Brown, 2000)

解读财务信息——这是所有会计人员应具备的最重要技能之一。任何交易或一系列事件只有一个解释是非常罕见的。因此，在进行调查时，法务会计师必须能够识别和解释与调查欺诈行为有关的所有财务信息。(Singleton & Singleton, 2010; Harris & Brown, 2000)

All these skills as described by Singleton & Singleton (2010) are also mentioned in study conducted by Harris & Brown (2000). Harris and Brown (2000) have classified specialized skills and technical abilities of forensic accountants. Forensic accountants are usually aware with criminal and civil law and comprehend courtroom procedures and expectations (Harris & Brown, 2000). Grippo & Ibex (2003) explained that the most fundamental skills of forensic accountants come from their experience in accounting, auditing, taxation, internal controls, interpersonal relationships, business operations, management and communication. Therefore, all the scholars like Harris & Brown (2000), Messmer (2004) and Ramaswamy (2005) who conducted studies related to skills required by forensic accountants, have mentioned more or less same set of skills as proposed in Singleton & Singleton（2010）.

Harris & Brown（2000）进行的研究也提到了 Singleton & Singleton（2010）描述的所有这些技能。Harris 和 Brown（2000）对司法会计师的专业技能和技术能力进行了分类。法务会计师通常了解刑法和民法，了解法庭程序和期望获得的证据（Harris & Brown，2000）。Grippo 和 Ibex（2003）解释说，法务会计师最基本的技能来自他们在会计、审计、税务、内部控制、人际关系、商业运作、管理和沟通方面的经验。因此，Harris 和 Brown（2000）、Mcssmer（2004）和 Ramaswamy（2005）等学者在进行与法务会计师所需技能相关的研究时，都或多或少提到了 Singleton 和 Singleton（2010）中提出的一套技能。

2.3.2 Required Competencies of the Forensic Accountants to be qualified for the role 法务会计师必须具备胜任这一职务的能力

The required skills set of a forensic accountant mentioned above are more or less taken from academic literature from forensic accounting courses and practitioners in practice. DiGabriele（2008）in his study has identified the views of all three main stakeholders-accounting academics, forensic accounting practitioners, and users of forensic accounting. From the views of all of them, DiGabriele（2008）has identified different competencies required by forensic accountants：

上述法务会计的必备技能，或多或少都是从法务会计课程的学术文献和实务中汲取的。DiGabriele（2008）在他的研究中确定了三个主要利益相关者—会计学者、法务会计从业人员和法务会计用户的观点。DiGabriele（2008）从所有这些人的角度，确定了法务会计师需要具备的不同能力：

· Deductive analysis, which seems to be vital for forensic accountants to uncover any potential financial scams.

·演绎分析，这对法务会计师发现任何潜在的财务欺诈似乎至关重要。

· Critical thinking, an ability to interpret differences between beliefs and facts.

·批判性思维，解释信念和事实之间差异的能力。

· Unstructured problem solving.

·解决非结构化问题的能力。

· Investigative flexibility, an ability to adopt different investigative techniques to examine situations than traditional and standardized audit procedures.

调查灵活性，采用不同于传统和标准化审计程序的调查技术来审查情况的能力。

· Analytical proficiency, an ability to differentiate and analyse between available information and information to be sought.

·分析能力，能够区分和分析可用信息和要查找的信息。

· Oral communication.

口头交流。

· Written communication.

·书面表达。

· Specific legal knowledge, an ability to recognize different legal matters in case of expert testimony to be provided.

·具体的法律知识，在提供专家证词的情况下识别不同法律事项的能力。

· Composure, an ability to maintain a relaxed and calm attitude in tensed situations.

·镇定，在紧张局势中保持放松和平静态度的能力。

DiGabriele（2008）further grouped all these competencies into two main groups—knowledge ability and performance. The findings of DiGabriele research suggested that the three main stakeholder groups – accounting practitioners, accounting academics, and users of forensic accounting services have different opinions on all of knowledge and skill items but agree on all of the performance items. It was also proved in his research that accounting practitioners and accounting academics agreed on more important forensic competencies over users of forensic accounting services (DiGabriele, 2008).

DiGabriele（2008）进一步将所有这些能力分为两大类—知识能力和绩效。DiGabriele 研究发现，会计从业人员、会计学者和法务会计服务使用者这三个主要利益相关者群体对所有知识和技能项目有不同意见，但对所有绩效项目意见一致。他的研究还证明，会计从业人员和会计学者对法务会计服务使用者更重要的司法能力达成一致意见（DiGabriele，2008）。

2.3.3 Required Personalities traits for the Forensic Accountants 法务会计师必须具备的人格特质

According to American Institute of Certified Public Accountants (AICPA), the characteristics forensic accountants could be categorised in communication skills, analytical characteristics and investigative skills (AICPA, 2006). Harris & Brown (2000) bear also identified specialized skills, characteristics and technical abilities of forensic accountants. It is also believed that forensic accountants generally possess knowledge of criminal and civil law and apprehend the knowledge of courtroom procedures and expectations (DiGabriele, 2008). This also supports the AICPA view regarding categorization of characteristics in investigative skills, including theories, methods, and patterns of fraud abuse. This gives them ability to think out of the box and anticipate the tactics that a fraud perpetrator might use to commit and conceal illegal acts (DiGabriele, 2008). They should be adaptive and team player as well to different situations as they have to communicate with different departments regarding their findings as well as fraudulent activities, which are committed in the organization (DiGabriele,

2008）. According to Singleton & Singleton（2010）, the forensic accountants should posses characteristics which are different from traditional accountants. They should have qualities like:

据美国注册会计师协会（AICPA）介绍，法务会计师的特点可以分为沟通能力、分析能力和调查能力（AICPA，2006）。Harris 和 Brown（2000）还确定了法务会计师的专业技能、特点和技术能力。另据认为，法务会计师一般具有刑法和民法知识，了解法庭程序和期望（DiGabriele，2008）。这也支持 AICPA 关于调查技能特征分类的观点，包括欺诈滥用的理论、方法和模式这使他们有能力跳出框框，预见诈骗犯可能用来实施和隐瞒非法行为的策略（DiGabriele，2008）。他们应该适应不同的情况并且具有团队精神，因为他们必须与不同的部门沟通，了解他们的发现以及在组织中实施的欺诈活动（DiGabriele，2008）。根据 Singleton & Singleton （2010）的说法，法务会计师应该具有不同于传统会计师的特点。他们应该具备以下素质：

· Creativity, an ability to consider alternative business situations in normal business sense.

· 创造力，在正常商业意义上考虑替代商业情况的能力。

· Curiosity, the aspiration to discover what has taken place in given set of conditions.

· 好奇心，发现特定条件下发生的事情的愿望。

· Perseverance, an ability to push forth into investigative mind set even if documents and other conditions fully satisfy that there is no need to investigate.

· 坚持不懈，即使文件和其他条件完全满足不需要调查，也能继续推进调查的心态。

· Common sense and confidence.

· 常识和信心。

· Skepticism and inquisitive, an ability to prevent natural tendency to prejudge.

·怀疑和好奇，防止预先判断的自然倾向的能力。

Harris & Brown（2000）have also mentioned that forensic accountants should be analytical and evaluative; should function well under pressure; have the ability to generate new ideas and scenarios; should always be detail oriented and insightful; always intuitive and responsive to never faced set feel more friendly while interviewing or working with them in fraudulent activities case. Thus by combining the qualities mentioned by both Harris & Brown and Singleton & Singleton, one can come to an extensive set of skills and traits, a forensic accountant should be posses, which are as follows:

Harris 和 Brown（2000）也提到，法务会计师应该具有分析能力和评估能力，应在压力下工作良好，有能力产生新的想法和场景，应始终注重细节和洞察力。在欺诈活动中，面谈或与他们一起工作时，总是对从未面对过的场景有直觉和反应并感觉更友好。因此，结合 Harris 和 Brown 和 Singleton 和 Singleton 可以得出一套广泛的技能和特点，法务会计师应该具备如下素质：

·Analytical 分析能力

·Creativity 创造力

·Curiosity 好奇心

·Perseverance 毅力

·Skepticism and inquisitive 怀疑和好奇心

·Detail oriented and insightful 细节导向和洞察力

·Ability to work under pressure 在压力下工作的能力

Thus, this extensive set to a certain extent is a combination of personality traits and skills gained with time and training.

因此，这种广泛的设置在一定程度上是个性特征和随着时间和训练而获得的技能的结合。

Section 2.1 through 2.3 highlighted some of the necessities of a forensic accountant as mentioned in literature. The extensive list of traits clearly no test that Forensic accounts can be trained, but there are certain personality traits that make some people more suitable for the job than others.

第 2.1 至 2.3 节强调了文献中提到的法务会计师的一些必要性。大量的特征显然没有检验法务会计师是否可以训练，但有一些性格特征使一些人比其他人更适合这项工作。

2.4 The Expert Witnesses 专家证人

Lawyers, judges and forensic accountants have a different perspective for expert witnessing. Lawyers would like expert witness to rebut the opposing party's expert witness. Judges would like an expert witness to reach a conclusion in less time, when the judge cannot arrive at the conclusion without expert's help and the forensic accountants would like expert witnesses to assist lawyers, judges and courts to understand financial disputed matters accurately（Telpner & Mostek, 2002）. According to Poynter （1997）, an expert witness is a person possessing deeper knowledge of concerned subject area than any other individual by reason of training or special education. Copeland（1993） has defined an expert witness as "one who by reason of education or specialized experience possesses superior knowledge regarding a subject about which persons having no particular training are incapable of forming an accurate opinion or deducing correct opinions"（Copeland, 1993）. According to Poynter（1997）, there are 4 major reasons to bring expert witnesses in the case:

律师、法官和法务会计师对专家作证有不同的看法。律师希望专家证人反驳对方的专家证人。法官希望专家证人在没有专家帮助法官无法得出结论的情况下，能在较短的时间内得出结论。法务会计师希望专家证人协助律师、法官和法院准确理解财务争议事项（Telpner & Mostek，2002）。根据 Poynter（1997），专家证人是指由于培训或特殊教育，对相关主题领域的了解比任何其他人都要深的人。Copeland（1993）将专家证人定义为"由于教育或专业经验而对没有受过专门训练的人无法形成准确意见或推断正确意见的某一主题拥有高超知识的人"。根据 Poynter（1997），该案有 4 个主要原因需要聘请专家证人：

　　· When expert testimony involves professionals indulged in malpractices or any fraudulent activities.

　　当专家证词涉及纵容不当行为或任何欺诈活动的专业人员时。

　　· When expert testimony involves technological issues, complex concerns or business problems like financial accounting frauds and they are beyond the understanding of layman.

　　当专家证词涉及技术问题、复杂问题或法务会计欺诈等业务问题，且超出外行人的理解时。

　　· To assist the jury as their opinion might help jury to take decision accurately.

　　协助陪审团，因为他们的意见可能有助于陪审团准确做出决定。

　　· When a client-attorney has a tactical reason for hiring expert witness.

　　当委托人律师有战术理由聘用专家证人时。

Expert witnesses help in expert testimony as they explain the logic of the mechanism involved; they give authoritative opinion and; they enlarge the importance of case（Poynter, 1997）. Therefore, an expert witness cannot be any individual who could be in the court room to present the testimony in any matter. It is the judge who decides whether the person handling testimony in court is well qualified enough to handle the court proceedings or not. They have present documents, their special knowledge, experience, training or skills pertaining to the case and testimony（Poynter, 1997）. These all are presented by an attorney to judge in the court room and opposing attorney has right to challenge their qualifications as their main goal is to diminish the jury's confidence in expert's opinion（Poynter, 1997）. The expert witnesses opinion is based on special skills, abilities, knowledge and their special characteristics. These all are tested in the court room. Therefore, they need a lot of work experience as well as related education in the field to persuade the jury or judge in the court room.

专家证人在解释所涉机制的逻辑时协助专家作证，他们给出权威意见；他们增强了案件的重要性（Poynter，1997）。因此，专家证人不能是可以在法庭上就任何事项作证的任何个人。由法官决定在法庭上处理证词的人是否有足够资格处理法庭诉讼。他们出示了与案件和证词有关的文件、专门知识、经验、培训或技能（Poynter，1997）。所有这些都是由一名律师为了法庭的审判而提出，对方律师有权质疑他们的资格，因为他们的主要目的是降低陪审团对专家意见的信心（Poynter，1997）。专家证人的意见基于他们特殊的技能、能力、知识及其特点。这些都是可以在法庭上测试出来的。因此，他们需要大量的工作经验和相关的专业教育来说服法庭上的陪审团或法官。

2.4.1 Required Skills for an Expert Witness
专家证人应具备的技能

Murphy（1993）stated that a standard expert witness is a detective, a teacher and an interpreter. Expert witnesses should be detail oriented, must examine the documents, evidences and information related to testimony in detail; should acquire a good understanding of the case and be able to teach the jury members court proceeding. They must be well enabled and able to communicate the information into legal language so that jury members can understand and reach a conclusion. The main job of the expert witnesses in the courtroom is to hold the interest of the jury members towards their presentation and findings and persuade them to believe it. One of the ways could be through describing methodology and the whole process of their investigation in which it was carried out. This could lead the jury members to accept their opinions. They are also good at assessing and eliminating unrelated information to the testimony. They are really good at distinguishing problems with which they are aware, proposing substitute resolutions and selecting worthy options among the substitutes（Feder, 1991）. Therefore, there has to be special knowledge, skills and abilities in an expert witness to turn around the case in the courtroom towards them. Poynter （1997）has stated following skills and abilities in the expert witnesses:

Murphy（1993）说，标准的专家证人是侦探、教师和翻译。鉴定人应当注重细节，必须详细审查与证言有关的文件、证据和资料，要对案件有较好的了解和把握，同时能够教授陪审团成员法庭诉讼程序。他们必须具备良好的能力，能够将信息转换成法律语言，以便陪审团成员理解并得出结论。法庭专家证人的主要工作是保持陪审团成员对他们陈述和调查结果的兴趣并说服他们相信这一点。其中一种方式可以是通过描述方法和进行调查的整个过程。这可能导致陪审团成员接受他们的意见。他们还善于评估和消除与证词无关的信息。他们真的很善于辨别他们意识到的问题，提出替代方案，并在替代方案中选择有价值的选择（Feder, 1991）。因此，一名专家证人要在法庭上把案件转交给他们，必须具备特殊的知识、技能和能力。Poynter（1997）陈述专家证人所具有的以下技能和能力：

· Analytical ability, which enable them to investigate the problems deeply.

分析能力，使他们能够深入调查问题。

· Inquisitive skills, which enable them to be the type of person who wants to, know why things happen. They love to find problems.

好奇的技能，使他们成为想知道事情发生原因的人。他们喜欢寻找问题。

· Reasoning skills and abilities, which enable them to handle hypothetical questions in the courtroom.

推理技能和能力，使他们能够在法庭上处理假设性问题。

· Mediagenic abilities, which enable them likable, exciting and convincing.

They have to make testimony interesting through their excellent communication skills.

媒体能力，让他们变得可爱、令人激动并令人信服。他们必须通过出色的沟通技巧使证词变得有趣。

·Prior experience, which enable them to boost confidence of the jury members in them, as they do not prefer virgin experts.

以往的经验使他们能够增强陪审团成员对他们的信心，因为他们不喜欢没有经验的专家。

·Public speaking ability, which enable them to speak freely. Good communications skills make them express their thoughts and respond quickly to defend their position. They should be able to break down complex issues to the jury members with the help simple examples.

公共演讲能力，使他们能够畅所欲言。良好的沟通技巧使他们表达自己的想法，并迅速做出反应来捍卫自己的地位。他们应该能够借助简单的例子把复杂的问题分解给陪审团成员。

·Ability to persuade others and teaching abilities.

说服他人的能力和教学能力。

·Writing abilities, which enable them to put their thoughts on paper. They have to sell their evidence in the courtroom to the jury members.

写作能力，使他们能够把想法写在纸上。他们必须在法庭上把证据呈现给陪审团成员。

While the academia provides a lost list of required skills for an expert witness Casey（2003）point out that there is a case law in the UK context to state the requirements for an expert which are as follows:

尽管学术界为专家证人提供了一份丢失的所需技能清单，但 Casey（2003）指出，英国有一项判例法，规定对专家的要求如下：

·Qualified in the respective field 在各自领域合格

· Non-Partisan 无党派

· Up-to-date with the current research 当前最新的研究

· Ability to provide the justification for opinion 提供意见理由的能力

· Ability to separate fact from opinion 能够将事实与意见分开

· Must have examined the defendant recently, if relevant 如果相关的话，最近一定检查过被告

These are the conditions an expert witness needs to satisfy to be considered credible by the court in England, Whales and Scotland.

在英格兰、威尔士和苏格兰，专家证人需要满足这些条件才能被法庭认为可信。

It is because of these skills of the expert witnesses that their interpretations are presented in the courtroom as opinions（Saks & Wissler, 1984）. But there should be some precautions that are to be kept in mind by expert witnesses during testimony. According to Pagano & Buckhoff（2005）, as sometimes expert's interpretations are taken as opinions, the source should be truthful and honestly verified before presenting them in the courtroom. Also, the qualifications and prior experience presented in court should not be overstated; otherwise it would be easily spotted through logic and common sense during testimony（Pagano & Buckhoff, 2005）.

正是由于专家证人的这些技巧，他们的解释才在法庭上被作为意见提出（Saks & Wissler，1984）。但是专家证人在作证时应该注意一些预防措施。根据 Pagano & Buckhoff（2005）的说法，由于有时专家的解释被视为意见，在法庭上陈述之前，消息来源应该是真实和诚实的。此外，在法庭上提出的资历和以往的经验不应被夸大。否则，在作证时很容易被人们用逻辑和常识识别出来（Pagano & Buckhoff，2005）。

2.4.2 Required Traits and Characteristics of an Expert Witness 鉴定人必须具备的特征和特点

According to various studies conducted by notable scholars (Wilkerson, 1997; Matson, 1999; Matkin, 1983; Bronstein, 1999; Freder, 1991; Iyer, 1993; Poytner, 1997; Faherty, 1995; Quigley, 1991; Berry, 1990; Weikel & Hughes, 1993), the following traits and characteristics of an expert witness are identified:

根据著名学者进行的各种研究 (Wilkerson, 1997; Matson, 1999; Matkin, 1983; Bronstein, 1999; Freder, 1991; Iyer, 1993; Poytner, 1997; Faherty, 1995; Quigley, 1991; Berry, 1990; Weikel & Hughes, 1993), 鉴定了专家证人的以下特点和特征：

Knowledge, Education, and Training – According to Wilkerson (1997), the expert witnesses should compulsorily have specialized knowledge, education and training in their concerned area of expertise is the most important characteristic. This is vital in order to satisfy the jury members and judge about the opinions presented by expert witnesses (Wilkerson, 1997). The expert witnesses should have academic credentials such as patents or inventions, advanced degrees, certifications, and doctorate in special areas of study (Wilkerson, 1997). This particular trait was also mentioned in Matson (1999). He described expert witnesses as extremely knowledgeable in their specific subject area with a high level of education and work experience. While this is a generic summary it is very important that an expert witness is providing insights in the sector they belong to and have expertise in. The advancements and knowledge discussed above should be in a particular sector for a particular case based on its needs. Thus, an expert witness providing his/her services in a civil dispute related to property case should have his/her expertise in this area.

知识、教育和培训——根据 Wilkerson (1997) 的说法，鉴定人必须具有专业知识，他们所涉及的专业领域的教育和培训是最重要的特点。这对陪审团成员和法官对专家证人提出的意见感到满意至关重要（Wilkerson，1997）。专家证人应具有特殊研究领域的专利或发明、高级学位、证书和博士学位等学术证书（Wilkerson，1997）。Matson（1999）也提到了这一特点。他说，专家证人在他们的特定学科领域非常有知识，具有很高的教育水平和工作经验。虽然这是一个一般性的总结，但专家证人在他们所属的领域提供见解和专业知识是非常重要的。以上讨论的进步和知识应该是基于特定情况的特定部门的需求。因此，在与财产案件有关的民事纠纷中提供服务的专家证人应具备这方面的专门知识。

Experience – Experience provides a legitimate groundwork to the expert witnesses. With the help of and making full use of it, they can build a base to persuade the jury members and judge. With their extensive experience in particular subject area, they can aid in understanding the facts of an example and may easily influence the parties involved in litigation. This fact was also supported in the study conducted by Matkin（1983）, which mentions possession of a degree of proficiency with experience in the field is mandatory for expert witnesses. This expertise can help the jury members and judge to understand most complicated matters in the courtroom. According to Bronstein（1999）, the characteristics of an expert witness include – knowledge, skills, experience, training and education. In order to qualify as an expert witness, theoretically, an individual needs either one of them but most expert witnesses hold all of them. This provides them strong base for providing opinions in courtrooms against their interpretations. These were also proved in studies conducted by Feder（1991）and Iyer（1993）. It was furthermore added by these notable scholars that the expert witnesses should also have the teaching, writing and communication skills and abilities, which will help the parties involved in testimony to quickly understand the issues. As mentioned before the required traits and skills can be obtained by training but it is very essential for an expert to have gained knowledge through experience thus making the experience more practical and valuable. In the literature, some authors are also arguing about the need for experts to have teaching experience thus point to those individuals in practice to have a touch with academia as well.

经验——经验为专家证人提供了合理的基础。借助并充分利用经验，他们可以建立一个基础来说服陪审团成员和法官。凭借他们在特定领域的丰富经验，他们可以帮助理解一个例子的事实，并且很容易影响诉讼当事人。Matkin（1983）进行的研究也证实了这一事实，其中提到，专家证人必须具备一定程度的实地经验。这种专业知识可以帮助陪审团成员和法官理解法庭上最复杂的事情。Bronstein（1999）认为，专家证人的特点包括知识、技能、经验、培训和教育。理论上，一个人要具备专家证人的资格，要么需要其中一个，但大多数专家证人都持有这些证据。这为他们在法庭上提出反对其解释的意见提供了坚实的基础。Feder（1991）和 Iyer（1993）进行的研究也证明了这一点。这些著名学者还补充说，专家证人还应具备教学、写作和交流的技能和能力这将有助于参与作证的各方迅速了解问题。如前所述，所需的特质和技能可以通过培训获得，但专家通过经验获得知识非常重要从而使经验更加实用和有价值。在文献中，也有一些作者认为专家需要有教学经验并指出在实践中专家也需要与学术界接触。

Investigative orientation–Poynter（1997）has indicated that inquisitiveness as one of the foremost qualities of the expert witnesses which extinguishes them to find problems rather than waiting for the problem to be found out. This trait will provide them inspiration to extensively examine investigate fraudulent matters（Poynter, 1997）. It was furthermore added by Poynter （1997） that the expert witnesses evaluates all possible alternatives, whether in theory or in defense, investigate the event in detail, govern the tests and put all of them in written report to discuss the findings while presenting testimony in the court room. Expert witness should have the ability to be inquisitive about the data and only then will the opinion of the Expert Witness be critical more than just a presentation of the data.

调查取向 –Poynter（1997）指出，好奇心是专家证人的首要素质之一，它使他们不再等待问题被发现，而是去寻找问题。这一特点将激励他们广泛调查欺诈事件。Poynter（1997）进一步补充说，专家证人评估所有可能的替代方案，无论是在理论上还是在辩护中，对事件进行详细调查，管理测试，并在法庭上陈述证词时将所有这些方案写成书面报告以讨论调查结果。专家证人应该有对数据好奇的能力，只有这样，专家证人的意见而非对数据的陈述才是至关重要的。

Ability to formulate an objective opinion – Expert witnesses have to make opinions with their expertise knowledge in the area based on false set of facts. They do not have any personal knowledge of the facts and therefore, they are able to provide impartial view based on assumed set of facts. According to Quigley（1991）, expert witnesses should be professionals for either the appellant or for the defendant. Therefore, it is very important for them to form an objective opinion and should be expert in formulating and convincing the judge and jury about the facts they have assumed. Berry（1990）also supports the fact and furthermore added that the instant evaluation of clients and making further assumptions instantly at the hearing is vital for the expert witnesses. Furthermore, Weikel & Hughes（1993）suggested that the expert witnesses should be well prepared for providing their unbiased opinions after deeply investigating and evaluating relevant information and evidences carefully. An opinion should be formed on scientific fact, knowledge in the field, and evaluation of the subject.

形成客观意见的能力——专家证人必须以他们在该领域的专门知识根据一套错误的事实提出意见。他们对事实没有任何个人知识，因此能够根据假设的一组事实提供公正的看法。Quigley（1991）认为，专家证人应该是上诉人或被告的专业人员。因此，对他们来说，形成一个客观的意见是非常重要的，他们应该是专家，能够让法官和陪审团相信他们所假设的事实。Berry（1990）也支持这一事实并补充说，对当事人进行即时评估并在听证会上立即作出进一步假设，对专家证人至关重要。此外，Weikel 和 Hughes（1993）建议，专家证人在对相关信息和证据进行深入调查和评估后，做好提供公正意见的准备并应该对科学事实、实地知识和对这一课题的评价形成自己的意见.

Credibility- There is always a deep concern about credibility of information presented by the expert witnesses in testimony. This is because the opinions, which are provided by the expert witnesses during testimony, are always based on the assumed facts and evidences. Therefore, there will always be contradiction and decision makers – the judge and the jury members, will always evaluate the information and evidences against the veracity of the opposing party's information and evidences. It has to be credible enough to believe. Feder（1991）says– "Credibility is comprised of believability, integrity, credentials, ability, experience, honesty, sincerity, objectivity, and consistency". A study conducted by Weikel & Hughes（1993）also mentions credibility as one of the important traits in the expert witnesses. This could be achieved through special knowledge, well prepared about the testimony, opinions based on scientific facts and professional approach towards approaching problems. An Expert Witness should be able to demonstrate these so as to provide a strong foundation to his/her testimony and be able to sustain the cross-examination. A lack of these will see the expert witness testimony discarded wreaking the case.

可信度——专家证人在证词中提供的信息的可信度一直备受关注。这是因为专家证人在作证时提供的意见总是基于假设的事实和证据。因此，总会有矛盾，决策者——法官和陪审团成员——总会对照对方的信息和证据的真实性来评估信息和证据。它必须足够可信才能相信。Feder（1991）说：

信誉包括信任、正直、信用、能力、经验、诚实、真诚、客观和一致性。Weikel 和 Hughes（1993）进行的一项研究也提到可信度是专家证人的重要特征之一。这可以通过专门的知识、对证词的充分准备并基于科学事实的观点和对待问题的专业方法来实现。专家证人应该能够证明这些以便为他/她的证词提供坚实的基础并能够维持盘问。如果没有这些证据，专家证人的证词就会被抛弃，从而引发案件。

Ability to provide consistent testimony-Credibility and consistent testimony are interrelated. If the opinions of an expert witness keep on changing and not being in consistent during testimony, it will also reflect that the sources of information and evidence presented in testimony are not credible and the opposing party will have the benefit of this situation（Feder, 1991）. Therefore, it is very important to be consistent during testimony because the role of expert witness sometimes requires teaching as well and it will also help the judge and the jury members to understand the complex situations. It is established through expert witness' assertiveness, professionalism and communication abilities. According to Faherty（1995）, the expert witnesses should have the ability to provide consistent testimony by retaining a being assertive and using a well-modulated voice. The speech should be slow, clear, and natural.

提供一致证词的能力——可信度和一致证词是相互关联的。如果专家证人的意见在作证期间不断变化，不能保持一致，也将反映证词中提供的信息和证据来源不可信，对方将受益于这种情况（Feder, 1991）。因此，在作证时保持一致是非常重要的，因为专家证人的角色有时也需要教导，这也有助于法官和陪审团成员了解复杂的情况。它是通过专家证人的自信、专业和沟通能力建立的。Faherty（1995）认为，专家证人应该有能力通过保持自信和使用协调一致的声音来提供一致的证词。演讲应该缓慢、清晰、自然。

2.5 Requirements for an Expert Witness within Forensic Accounting 法务会计专家证人要求

It is very common that forensic accountants after finding about financial frauds resolve them before taking the matter into the courtroom. However, if the matter is to be taken into courtrooms for testimony, it has to be an expert witness presenting the testimony in the courtroom. The forensic accountants can testify themselves as expert witnesses and help the judges and juries to reach a conclusion to resolve the case as they do not have specialized knowledge as expert witnesses possess.（Okoye & Akamobi, 2009）. The advantage is provided to forensic accountants to resolve the disputes as an expert witness established on their knowledge and experience. However, according to Heighter & Heighter（2008）, there is neither any structured rules nor set of strong criteria for forensic accountants to act as expert witnesses in the courtroom. Therefore, it was argued by Harrison（2001）that there should be some specific guidelines and requirements for them to be professional in the courtrooms while presenting the testimony. This led scholars to research in this arena of forensic accounting.

法务会计师在发现财务欺诈后，在将此事提交法庭审理之前，通常会先解决这些问题。但是，如果要将此事带进法庭作证，那么必须是在法庭上作证的专家证人。法务会计人员由于具备专家证人所具备的专业知识，可以作为专家证人出庭作证，帮助法官和陪审团作出解决案件的结论。（Okoye 和 Akamobi, 2009）。法务会计人员凭借自己的知识和经验，作为专家证人解决纠纷更具有优势。然而，据 Heighter 和 Heighter（2008）说，法庭上没有任何有条理的规则，也没有一套强有力的标准让法务会计在法庭上充当专家证人。因此，Harrison（2001）认为，在提交证词时，他们在法庭上应该有一些专业的具体准则和要求。这促使学者们在法务会计领域进行研究。

DiGabriele（2010）suggested that objectivity and transparency are two vital indicators to assist forensic accountants in providing expert witness services. Rasmussen & Leauanae (2004) suggested academic qualifications, professional training, years of experience and charisma with good communication skills make forensic accountants distinctive in providing expert witness services. Heitger & Heitger (2008) also supported the suggestion made by Rasmussen & Leauanae (2004) by further adding specialised knowledge related auditing and the legal system and the professional certificates acquired in the forensic accounting realm.

Telpner & Mostek (2002) also suggests that forensic accountants providing expert witness services should be:

DiGabriele（2010）建议，客观性和透明度是协助法务会计师提供专家证人服务的两个重要指标。Rasmussen 和 Leauanae（2004）建议，学历、专业培训、多年的经验和魅力以及良好的沟通技巧使法务会计师在提供专家证人服务方面具有独特性。Heitger 和 Heitger（2008）还支持 Rasmussen 和 Leauanae（2004）提出的建议，进一步增加与审计相关的专业知识、法律制度以及在法务会计领域获得的专业证书。

Telpner 和 Mostek （2002）还建议，提供专家证人服务的法务会计师应该是：

· Diplomat – independent of the parties to the dispute.

外交官——独立于争议各方。

· Able to demonstrate proof of interpretations made by them。

能够证明他们做出的解释。

· Able to demonstrate teaching abilities as accounting is a complex subject and judges and jury will not be able to understand quickly in order to reach a conclusion.

能够证明教学能力，因为会计是一门复杂的学科，法官和陪审团无法快速理解以便得出结论。

However, the judges and the jury members may doubt on evidences presented by forensic accountants in testimony. Harrison（2001）and DiGabriele（2010） have argued in their studies that forensic accountants can be impartial and can compromise their objectivity as they render dual roles— litigation consultant and expert witness. Therefore, Lawrence（1998） suggested that there should be a control measure for entrance into this field, which can be applied through educational innovation and stringent rules regarding experience gained in this field. As the literature explains, the various services that forensic accountants undertake are very broad and complex. Thus, it is recommended for further more research for requirements and skill sets for forensic accountants as expert witnesses.

但是，法官和陪审团成员可能会对法务会计师在作证时提供的证据产生疑问。Harrison（2001）和 DiGabriele（2010）在他们的研究中认为，法务会计可以是公正的，并且在扮演诉讼顾问和专家证人双重角色时会损害他们的客观性。为此，Lawrence（1998）提出，应该有一个进入这一领域的控制措施，可以通过教育创新和严格的经验规则来实施。正如文献所解释的那样，法务会计所承担的各种服务是非常广泛和复杂的。因此，建议进一步研究法务会计师作为专家证人的要求和技能。

While the list of personality traits of individual combined with skills have been presented in the above sections Casey（2003） argues that experts until recently have gained the necessary Skills via experience only as there was a lack of training and accreditations necessary. This point stands corrected in todays date with various organizations like "The academy of Experts" and "Royal Institute of Charted Surveyors" and other professional institutions（See Appendix C）providing training to individuals to be experts. This is also supplemented with various academic institutions providing professional and academic courses on expert witness certification in the UK.

　　虽然个人的个性特征与技能结合的列表已经在上面的章节中介绍过，Casey（2003）认为，直到最近，专家都是通过经验获得了必要的技能，只是因为缺乏必要的培训和认证。这一点在今天已得到纠正，各种组织如"专家学院""皇家海图测量研究所"和其他专业机构（见附录C）向个人提供专家培训。除此之外，英国还有各种学术机构提供专家证人认证专业和学术课程。

　　Pagano & Buckhoff（2005）suggest that professionals taking proactive steps to be expert witnesses in their field should take following commandments while appearing in testimony:

　　Pagano & Buckhoff（2005）建议，采取主动行动成为本领域专家证人的专业人士在作证时应遵守戒律:

　　·The expert witness should not try to make up things in testimony. Tell the truth and give expert advice on what should be done.

　　专家证人不应试图在证词中捏造事实。说实话，并就应该做的事提出专家建议。

　　·Although academic credentials are important in this field but a person should have enormous experience as well in order to handle the testimony and able to teach the judge and the jury members in case of complicated testimonies.

　　虽然学历在这一领域很重要，但一个人也应该有丰富的经验来处理证词，并能够在证词复杂的情况下教导法官和陪审团成员。

　　·Never let the attorneys screen out the information. An expert witness within forensic accounting should do its homework and try to communicate it properly to participants in testimony.

　　切勿让律师筛选出信息。法务会计领域的专家证人应做应做之事，并将它正确传达给证人。

　　·Maintain control over documents. An expert witness should always know that from where the information is being fed and should always know the fundamental base for information to be given out.

保持对文件的控制。专家证人应该始终知道信息是从哪里提供的，应该始终知道提供信息的基本依据。

· An expert witness should always use visual presentations and should have excellent communication skills. They should always be deeper and loud enough in testimonies as the matter may be very complicated to understand due its accounting nature.

专家证人应始终使用视觉演示，并应具有出色的沟通技巧。他们的证词应该总是足够深刻和响有影响力，因为由于其会计性质，事情可能非常复杂，难以理解。

· Never personally attack the other person in testimony. An expert witness within forensic accounting should be able to deal professionally without hurting any other person's emotions during testimony.

切勿亲自攻击他人作证。法务会计领域的专家证人在作证时，应能在不伤害他人感情的情况下进行专业处理。

2.6　Hypotheses 假设

Based on the thorough literature review and studies, the following hypotheses for requirements for an expert witness to be self-sufficient in forensic accounting are deduced for further testing in this research:

在全面文献回顾和研究的基础上，本文推导出了充分成为在法务会计领域的专家证人的要求的假设，以供本研究进一步检验：

H1 – Forensic Accountant in expert witnessing should have extensive knowledge, be professionally trained and high academic qualifications as its characteristics.

H1——鉴定人见证中的法务会计应具有广博的知识，经过专业培训，具有较高的学历作为其特点。

H2 – Forensic Accountant should have diplomat skills and excellent communication skills to be an expert witness.

H2——法务会计应具备外交技巧和良好的沟通技巧，才能成为专家证人。

H3 – Forensic accountant should possess skeptic, investigative, detailed orientation and analytical abilities as its competencies to be able to self-sufficient in expert witnessing.

H3——法务会计应具备怀疑、调查、详细定位和分析能力，作为其能够进行专家见证的能力。

2.7 Conclusion 结论

To conclude, Forensic accountants are the experts who have extensive experience in investigations to determine solutions to disputed financial fraud matters. These abilities are not natural born in forensic accountants, but it comes with their specialized knowledge of the field, skills, competencies, traits and characteristics, which are developed over a period of time. These forensic accountants also help organizations by playing the role of expert witness during the courtroom testimonies related to financial fraud cases running in courts. To be an expert witness, the forensic accountant should adopt special skills, abilities, traits and characteristics of an expert witness in order to persuade judge, and the jury members about the their opinions, which are based on assumed facts and figures found during the investigation. This research report focuses on requirements of an expert witness to be self-sufficient within forensic accounting arena during the presentation of testimony. The requirements are proposed through hypotheses, which are created by doing secondary research from various literature studies and books written by scholars in the area forensic accounting and expert witnessing. These hypotheses would be tested through a research process and appropriate methodology, which is further continued in the next chapter.

综上所述，法务会计师是具有丰富调查经验的专家，能够解决有争议的财务欺诈问题。这些能力不是法务会计天生的，而是随着一段时间的发展而形成的专业知识、技能、能力、特征和特点。这些法务会计师还通过在法庭上充当与法庭审理的财务欺诈案件有关的证词的专家证人来帮助组织机构。作为专家证人，法务会计应根据调查中发现的假设事实和数字，采用专家证人的特殊技能、能力、特征和特点，说服法官和陪审团成员听取他们的意见。本研究报告着重探讨了足以成为法务会计领域的专家证人在作证期间的要求。这些要求是通过假设提出的，这些假设是通过对各种文献研究以及法务会计和专家见证领域学者撰写的书籍进行二次研究而产生的。这些假设将通过研究过程和适当的方法进行检验，这将在下一章继续进行。

CHAPTER
III

Research
Methodology

第三章 / 研究方法

3.1 Introduction 导言

According to Kothari（2006）, Research Methodology is defined as "the way to systematically solve a research problem." Importantly, it is different between Research methodology and research methods. Research method means a logical way that is used by a researcher for a subject matter investigation. It is important to choose appropriate techniques and research methods which are more suitable than others. The combination of techniques and methods used in a particular subject is research methodology. This section provides a description for the relevant research methods that were used in order to critically evaluate and analyze the literature review and assist in achieving the investigation's prior aims and objectives.

根据Kothari（2006），研究方法被定义为"系统解决研究问题的方法"。重要的是，研究方法论和研究方法不同。研究方法是指研究人员用于主题调查的逻辑方式。选择合适的技术和研究方法是非常重要的，这些技术和研究方法比其他技术和方法更适合。特定学科所用的技术和方法的结合是研究方法论。本节介绍了为批判性地评价和分析文献综述并帮助实现调查的先前目标和任务而使用的相关研究方法。

3.2 Research Methodology 研究方法

According to White（2002）, Research Methodology is the rational, logical and theoretical basis on which research has been founded. Therefore, this plays very important part in any research. But in some studies, the "Methodology", "Data Collection" and descriptions of methods are disengaged. It has been argued to be the main problem of some researches（Cameron & Price

2009）. Thus, a person carrying out research should first understand different epistemologies, to think about different epistemologies, research perspective and then accordingly research strategy and data gathering techniques should be used （Cameron & Price, 2009）.

White（2002）认为，研究方法是研究的理性、逻辑和理论基础。因此，这在任何研究中都起着非常重要的作用。但在一些研究中，"方法论""数据收集"和对方法的描述是脱节的。有人认为这是一些研究的主要问题（Cameron & Price, 2009 ）。因此，进行研究的人应该首先理解不同的认识论，思考不同的认识论、研究视角，然后相应地运用研究策略和数据收集技术（Cameron & Price，2009 ）。

Research epistemologies are concerned with the nature and extent of knowledge, which will help in finding relevant research design and methods for conducting research （Cameron & Price, 2009）. There are 4 types of research epistemologies （Cameron & Price, 2009）:

研究认识论关注知识的性质和范围，这将有助于找到相关的研究设计和研究方法（Cameron & Price，2009）。研究认识论有四种类型（Cameron & Price, 2009）:

· **Positivism** – It is concerned with a belief that facts and figures exist independently of the observer, and can be verified through personal observation.

实证主义——它关注的是相信事实和数字独立于观察者而存在，并且可以通过个人观察得到验证。

· **Updated Realism** – It is concerned with a belief that although facts and figures may occur independently, but cannot be verified through direct observation.

更新的现实主义——它关注的是这样一种信念，即尽管事实和数字可能独立发生，但无法通过直接观察得到验证。

· **Pragmatism** – It is concerned with a belief in the complexity of situations, linked to a belief in many perspectives mentioned above.

实用主义——它关注对复杂情况的信念，与对上述许多观点的信念相关联。

· **Constructionism**-It is associated with a belief that those involved in project construct both facts as well as figures attributed to research.

建构主义——它与一种信念相关联，即参与项目的人既建构事实，也建构归因于研究的数字。

· Upon deciding about epistemology, the next step in research methodology is to select and decide on research perspective, which will provide an outline for the collection and analysis of data. According to Cameron & Price（2009），there are 2 types of research perspective:

在决定认识论时，研究方法的下一步是选择和决定研究视角，这将为收集和分析数据提供一个大纲。根据 Cameron 和 Price（2009），有两种研究视角：

· **Inductive** - This approach starts with opinions from involved parties and derives theories from those opinions.

归纳——这种方法始于有关各方的意见，并从这些意见中得出理论。

· **Deductive** - This approach starts with a detailed literature review on topic and deduces hypotheses from it. The hypotheses are later tested in research with careful measurement and sophisticated statistics.

演绎——这种方法从详细的主题文献综述开始，并从中演绎假设。这些假设后来在研究中通过仔细测量和精密统计得到验证。

Based on approach, the further step in research methodology is decided upon the most research strategy to be followed in research. Bryman and Bell（2011）have classified them in 2 categories:

在此基础上，研究方法的进一步发展决定了研究中最需要遵循的研究策略。Bryman 和 Bell（2011）将其分为两类。

· **Quantitative** – This strategy follows deductive approach to find out connection between academic theory and conducted research. It generally incorporates positivism epistemology and use surveys, questionnaires etc. as a tool to gather data from involved parties in research.

定量——这一策略遵循演绎方法，以发现学术理论与从事的研究之间的联系。它一般包括实证认识论和使用调查、问卷等，作为从参与研究的各方收集数据的工具。

· **Qualitative** – This strategy follows an inductive approach to find out connection between academic theory and conducted research. It uses interviews, participant observations etc. as a tool to gather data from involved parties in research.

定性——这一策略遵循归纳方法，以发现学术理论与已进行的研究之间的联系。它采用访谈、参与者观察等方式，作为从参与研究的各方收集数据的工具。

Both strategies could incorporate constructionism epistemology as well based on aims and objectives of research（Bryman & Bell, 2011）. According to the strategy, later, the type of data for collection will be decided. It could be either primary or secondary. Primary data, also termed as raw data, is collected for the current research for specific purpose, aims and objectives. Secondary data, whereas, has been collected and documented prior to the current research and it was originally collected for other purposes（Bryman & Bell, 2011）.

这两种策略都可以包含建构主义认识论，也可以基于研究的目标和任务（Bryman & Bell, 2011）。根据该策略，以后将决定收集的数据类型。它可以是初级数据也可以是二手数据。初级数据也称为原始数据，是为当前的研究而收集的，用于特定的目的、目标和任务。二手数据则是在本次研究之前收集和记录的，最初是为了其他目的而收集的（Bryman & Bell，2011）。

3.3 Research Methodology of This Research
本研究的研究方法

This paper is more of a positivist epistemology, as previously described (Bryman & Bell, 2011) existing figures and knowledge are verified via exiting academic literature and thereafter hypotheses will be deduced and tested. In particular, the study examines a preliminary analysis of skills, competencies and characteristics of the forensic accountants and expert witnesses from academic literature available and then uses quantitative method of data collection –a self-administered questionnaire, where all data gathered will be compared to the existing literature. Although relevant literature studies mention about forensic accountant being an expert witness but not much of the research has been done in this area. Therefore, it is important to review and extend research in this area, which would help forensic accountants in the courtroom as an expert witness. The research will be deductive in nature. The quantitative strategy would be used for collecting data from participants and the collected data would be analyzed mathematically in SPSS with various statistical tools. The quantitative strategy would be used and not qualitative because the past is a deductive system and provides an ideal base to support the academic literature, accept or reject the deduced hypotheses and provide a more impartial base to guide professional practice (White, 2002).

本文更多的是实证主义认识论，如前所述（Bryman & Bell，2011），现有的数字和知识通过现有的学术文献得到验证，然后假设将被推导和检验。特别是，这项研究从现有的学术文献中初步分析了法务会计师和专家证人的技能、能力和特点，然后使用数据收集的定量方法——一种自我管理的问卷，其中收集的所有数据将与现有文献进行比较。虽然相关文献研究中提到法务会计是专家证人，但这方面的研究并不多。因此，有必要对这一领域的研究进行回顾和拓展以帮助法庭上的法务会计人员作为专家证人。

这项研究将是演绎性质的。定量策略将用于收集参与者的数据，收集的数据将在 SPSS 中用各种统计工具进行数学分析。由于过去是一个演绎系统，为支持学术文献、接受或拒绝演绎的假设提供了理想的基础，并为指导专业实践提供了更公正的基础，因此将采用量化策略，而不是定性策略（White，2002）。

3.4 *Steps in Research Process 研究过程中的步骤*

According to Kumar （2011, Figure 2）, the whole research process is a step by step process and should be followed in a manner which is best possible described in below mentioned figure 2 （Kumar, 2011）:

Kumar（2011 年，图 2）认为，整个研究过程是一个逐步的过程，应该遵循下面提到的图 2 （Kumar，2011）中最可能描述的方式：

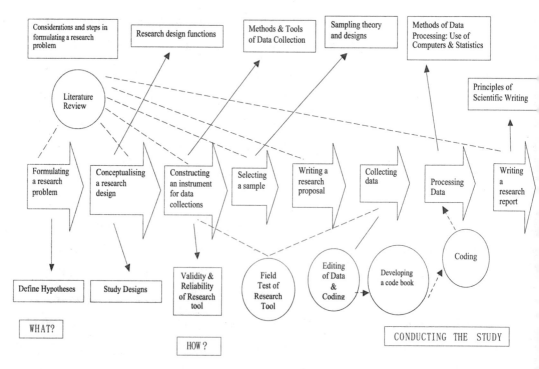

Figure 2 Steps in Research Process（adapted from Kumar（2011））

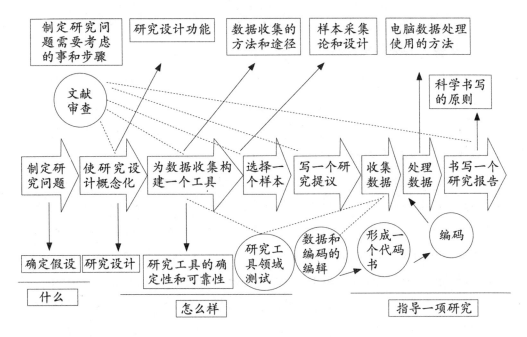

图2　研究过程中的步骤（改编自 Kumar（2011））

Step 1: Writing a research proposal
步骤：撰写研究报告

The research proposal mentions a refined and a more specific research problem, its main purpose, aims and objectives, hypotheses and research questions designed in a much more structured format. The most important aspect of research proposal is to look for relevant literature theoretical frameworks, studies or books, which has been already published in the concerned area. At this stage, the literature review is much more extensive and to the point of research's aims and objectives

研究方案提到了一个更精细、更具体的研究问题，其主要目的、目标和任务、假设和研究问题都是以更加结构化的形式设计的。研究方案最重要的方面是寻找相关的文献理论框架以及已经在相关领域发表的研究或书籍。现阶段，文献综述更加广泛，达到了研究的目标和任务。

Step 2: Formulating the research problem
步骤 2: 制定研究问题

This step will start with the preparation of a research idea. It will include introduction, aims and objectives and research methods to be followed in research. The research idea is related to the field of forensic accounting and expert witness and their characteristics, skills and competencies. This was then further developed based on a preliminary academic literature, discussions with director and various books related to the topic and therefore incorporated into the formal research proposal. Limited literature was found related to requirements for a forensic accountant to become an expert witness, and it was an area of paramount interest. Therefore, this leads to further detailed research in this area.

这一步将从准备研究思路开始。它将包括引言、目的和目标以及研究中应遵循的研究方法。研究思路涉及法务会计和专家证人及其特点、技能和能力。随后，在初步的学术文献、与指导者的讨论以及与该主题相关的各种书籍的基础上进一步发展，并吸收到正式的研究方案中。在此过程中发现有关要求法务会计师成为专家证人的文献有限，所以这个成为一个最重要的领域。因此，这就导致了这方面的内容需要进一步深入研究。

Step 3: Conceptualising a research design
步骤 3: 构思研究设计

In this step, based on the available academic literature, a straightforward approach was decided. It includes collection of related information through primary and secondary data. The majority of the secondary data was collected through forensic accounting journals and books, due to the nature of the topic. In addition quantitative data will be gathered through self-administered questionnaires, which would be the base for primary data.

在这一步中，根据现有的学术文献，确定了一种直接的方法。它包括通过原始数据和二手数据收集相关信息。由于课题的性质，大部分二手数据是通过法务会计期刊和书籍收集的。此外，将通过自我管理的问卷收集定量数据，这将是原始数据的基础。

Step 4: Constructing an instrument for data collection

步骤 4: 构建数据采集工具

Based on detailed analysis of literature review conducted, a short yet precise questionnaire was prepared. This research has been carried out with an intention to find the requirements for an expert witness to be sufficiently independent within the forensic accounting. It will look into different skills, competencies and characteristics of forensic accountants and expert witnesses. This needs to be measured because of following reasons:

在对文献综述进行详细分析的基础上，备制了一份简短而精确的问卷。这项研究的目的是要找到一名专家证人在法务会计中足够独立的要求。它将研究法务会计师和专家证人的不同技能、能力和特点。这些需要被衡量的原因如下：

· It can clearly present the variations in skills, competencies and characteristics of a forensic accountant and expert witness.

它可以清楚地展示法务会计师和专家证人的技能、能力和特征的差异。

· It will provide consistent results with respect to existing literature studies expert witness within forensic accounting.

它将提供关于法务会计领域关于专家证人现有文献研究的一致结果。

Therefore, on the basis of this, the self-administered questionnaire which contains 12 questions was designed for this research. It begins with classification questions aimed at obtaining information about participants, their profession, and level of education. Following to this, question 4 is regarding area（s） of specialty that a participant believes are appropriate for a forensic accountant and an expert witness. This was a multiple choice question, where a respondent can choose more than 1 are of speciality for both. Thereafter, following question 5, 6 and 7regard the skills, competencies and characteristics of a forensic accountant respectively. This were measured by responses on a five-point Likert scale of agreement, ranging from 1 = strongly disagree to 5 = strongly agree. The latter questions 8 and 9 followed with skills and characteristics of an expert witness respectively. The question 10 asks about the requirements for a forensic accountant to be an expert witness. All the Likert scale questions were formed from different academic literature studies, which were being discussed in the literature review section from different books and journal articles. Next question collects information from participants whether they ever played the role of an expert witness or not. The question 12 closes survey with asking participant's view on asking whether a forensic accountant can be an expert witness as well.

因此，在此基础上，问了本研究设计了包含 12 个问题的自评问卷。它从分类问题开始，旨在获取有关参与者的职业和教育水平的信息。随后，问题 4 涉及参与者认为适用于法务会计和专家证人的专业领域。这是一个多项选择的问题，被调查者可以选择 1 个以上，这两个问题都有其特殊性。此后，在问题 5、6 和 7 之后，分别涉及一名法务会计师的技能、能力和特点。这是通过在 5 点 Likert 同意量表上的反应来衡量的，从 1 = 强烈不同意到 5 = 强烈同意。后两个问题 8 和 9 分别是关于专家证人的技能和特点。问题 10 问及法务会计师作为专家证人的要求。所有的 Likert 量表问题都是由不同的学术文献研究形成的，文献综述部分从不同的书籍和期刊文章中讨论这些问题。下一个问题是从参与者那里收集信息，看他们是否扮演过专家证人的角色。问题 12 在调查结束时询问参与者对法务会计师能否也可以成为专家证人的看法。

Step 5: Sampling and Data Collecting
步骤 5：取样和数据收集

As the title of the research suggests about expert witness within forensic accounting, the area of research was specifically limited to forensic accountants and expert witnesses. But concerning about the limitations of time and the scope of the study, there were only people related to forensic accounting in UK was being contacted. Therefore, sampling practice has been applied. A sample is a subset of a larger population (Bryman & Bell, 2011). The purpose of sampling is to let researchers evaluate some unknown traits of the population and to generalize results from a sample to a population (Bryman & Bell, 2011). There are two ways of choosing samples - random (probability) sampling and non-random (non-probability) sampling (White, 2002). The method used for sampling in this research is a non-random sampling and more specifically-convenient sampling. According to White (2002), convenient sampling is a "type of non-probability sampling which involves the sample being drawn from that part of the population which is close to hand". It is used in this research because the details of forensic accountants, attorneys and expert witness were readily available and convenient through their own associations. One of the major limitations to this sampling technique is that it is very hard to generalize about the whole population as it would not be representative enough for the whole population due to its size. However, the reason being it was chosen is the accuracy of data as people who are involved in day to day forensic accounting services were made as participants for this research. The participants were the members selected from personal friends who work at the account firm. They were contacted through email by sending a link to the questionnaire. It was a self-administrated questionnaire sent by email indicating the link towards an online questionnaire. The online questionnaire was prepared on www.surveymonkey.

com, which allows researchers to create their own web-survey.

　　由于研究的题目是关于法务会计中的专家证人，所以研究的领域特别局限于法务会计和专家证人。但考虑到研究的时间和范围的限制，目前只联系到在英国与法务会计相关的人员。因此，采样实践得到了应用。样本是较大人口的子集（Bryman & Bell，2011）。抽样的目的是让研究人员评估一些未知的群体特征，并将抽样结果推广到一个群体（Bryman & Bell，2011）。有两种选择样本的方法——随机（概率）抽样和非随机（非概率）抽样（White，2002）。本研究采用的抽样方法是非随机抽样，特别是方便抽样。根据 White（2002）的说法，方便抽样是"一种非概率抽样，它涉及从易接近的那部分人群中抽取样本"。它被用于这项研究，因为法务会计师、律师和专家证人的详细资料可以通过他们自己的联系方便地获得。这种抽样技术的一个主要局限是很难对整个人口进行概括，因为由于它的规模对整个人口来说不够具有代表性。然而，之所以选择它，是因为数据的准确性，因为参与日常法务会计服务的人被选为这项研究的参与者。参与者是从在会计师事务所工作的个人朋友中挑选出来的成员。他们是通过电子邮件联系到问卷的。这是一份自我管理的问卷，通过电子邮件发送在线问卷的链接。网上问卷是在 www.surveymonkey.com 准备的，这使得研究人员可以创建自己的网络调查。

As previously mentioned, the data was collected from participants through a self-administered questionnaire link sent in an email to participants. There were more than 400 emails sent to participants email address, which was collected from association of forensic accountants, association of expert witness and London solicitor litigation association. Out of which 90 mails were failed delivered. This was due to data which is available on the website was not updated to date, or the person in charge was not on a desk or cannot be reached through email. This squeezed the number of respondents that would be available to participate. There were 3 reminders sent to participants to fill the questionnaire and in the end,

79 responses were received. The collected data is then downloaded to Microsoft excel format from survey monkey website.

如前所述，数据是通过发送给参与者的电子邮件中的自我管理问卷链接从参与者那里收集的。从司法会计师协会、专家证人协会和伦敦律师诉讼协会收集到 400 多封发给参与者的电子邮件地址。其中 90 封邮件投递失败。这是因为网站上提供的数据至今没有更新，或者负责人不在办公，或者无法通过电子邮件联系到。这压缩了可以参与的受访者人数。向与会者发出 3 份催复通知，填写调查表，最后收到 79 份答复。收集的数据然后从调查猴网站下载到 Microsoft Excel 格式。

Step 6: Processing Data
步骤 6：处理数据

Data received was processed through by firstly, exporting all collected responses to the Microsoft Excel application. As it was previously mentioned, this research report uses quantitative strategy; therefore, for analysis of data, researcher needs to transform collected responses into quantified data on which different analytical functions and statistical tools could be performed. Therefore, the responses are converted to quantified data as 1 = strongly disagree to 5 = strongly agree for question 6, 7, 8, 9 and 10. The other polar questions are quantified 1 = yes and 0 = no. It was difficult for quantifying "neutral" in Likert scale questions, but by following conservative approach, it was coded as 0. The quantified data from completed questionnaire of 79 respondents were saved in Excel spread sheet. This data was then uploaded to SPSS 20 programme. This programme is used for the quantitative data to be analysed and presented. The analysis was started with different frequency tables and statistical tools in SPSS.

接收到的数据首先通过将收集到的所有反馈导出到 Microsoft Excel 应用程序进行处理。如前所述，本研究报告采用定量策略。因此，为了分析数据，研究人员需要将收集到的反应转化为量化的数据，在这些数据上可以执行不同的分析功能和统计工具。因此，对于问题6、7、8、9和10，反馈被转换为量化数据，因为"1 = 强烈不同意"到"5 = 强烈同意"。其他的极性问题被量化为"1 = 是"和"0 = 否"。在Likert量表问题中，很难量化"中性"，但是按照保守的方法，它被编码为79名受访者填写的问卷量化数据保存在Excel电子表格中。这些数据随后被上传到SPSS 20程序。该程序用于分析和呈现定量数据。此分析从SPSS中的不同频率表和统计工具开始。

Step 7: Writing a research report
步骤7: 撰写研究报告

The last and most important step is to write the research report with all data collected, analyzed and present its findings with critically discuss with literature review. The research report starts with an introduction of research topic with its aims and objectives, covering literature review about skills, competencies and characteristics of the forensic accountants and expert witnesses in the next section, followed by research methodology, analysis and findings and concluding with critical analysis and conclusion with recommendations for a research topic.

最后也是最重要的一步，是撰写研究报告，收集、分析和呈现研究结果，并与文献综述进行批判性讨论。研究报告首先介绍了研究课题及其目的和目标，包括下一节对法务会计师和专家证人的技能、能力和特点的文献综述，然后介绍研究方法、分析和发现，最后进行批判性分析和结论并提出研究课题的建议。

3.5 Validity, Reliability, Research Ethics & Confidentiality
有效性、可靠性、研究伦理与保密性

It is very important to understand that whether the sample in research gives valid and reliable results for the whole population（Bryman & Bell, 2011）.

Validity is defined as an indicator which denotes whether research is measuring what it is supposed to measure or not（Bryman & Bell, 2011）. The higher level of validity could be achieved in quantitative data through primary research, which means the questionnaire should be based on frameworks, theories or literature proved and accepted by scholars in forensic accounting. Therefore, this research uses notes from several scholars.

　　了解研究中的样本是否为全体人口提供了有效可靠的结果是非常重要的（Bryman & Bell，2011）。有效性定义为一种指标，表示研究是否在衡量它应该衡量的东西（Bryman & Bell，2011）。通过初步研究，定量数据的效度可以达到较高的水平，这意味着调查问卷应该建立在法务会计学者所证实和接受的框架、理论或文献的基础上。因此，本研究使用了几位学者的笔记。

The reliability is basically associated with matters of uniformity of measures of concepts and will govern whether the conducted research is able to create impartial, unprejudiced results and analysis that reflect the reality. Bryman & Bell（2011）has stated that a reliable research is expected to be stable research. It should have to be same or at least similar results to those findings which was it was done by other scholars previously. It is also expected to be internally reliable. All the questions and options available in questions in the survey should be inter-connected and inter-related with each other（Bryman & Bell, 2011）. Therefore, in order to ensure the reliability, Cronbach's coefficient alpha test is used to measure internal consistency used in this research.

　　可靠性基本上与概念度量的一致性有关，将决定所进行的研究是否能够产生公正、不偏不倚的结果和反映现实的分析。Bryman & Bell（2011）表示，可靠的研究有望成为稳定的研究。它应该与其他学者以前的研究结果相同或至少相似。它还可望在内部可靠。调查中的所有问题和选项都应该是相互关联和相互关联的（Bryman & Bell，2011）。因此，为了保证可靠性，本研究采用 Cronbach 系数 alpha 检验来衡量内部一致性。

According to Bryman & Bell（2011）, ethical issues in any research into a state in which the role of values in the whole research process becomes an important topic of anxiety. It includes matters related to treatment of participants and their level of personal involvement with the research. Respecting the participants is the most vital part in any research and it could be only assured my respecting participant's confidentiality and anonymity. The conducting of this research was directed by ethical guidelines that aid to generate confidence and trust among participants and the researcher. Therefore, all the participants were made aware about the research topic with its aims and objectives in detail, in a cover letter sent to them in e-mail with questionnaire link. A participant information sheet was also attached in all e-mails sent to participants. It allowed participants to voluntarily take part in research. There were no personal questions like their name, age, gender address etc. asked to participants in this research. This has ensured the complete confidentiality for the participants in this research.

据 Bryman 和 Bell（2011）说，任何研究中的伦理问题，如果处于价值观在整个研究过程中的作用，都会成为一个令人焦虑的重要话题。它包括与参与者的待遇和他们个人参与研究的程度有关的事项。尊重参与者是任何研究中最重要的部分，本书只能保证尊重参与者的保密性和匿名性。这项研究的进行是由伦理准则指导的，这些准则有助于在参与者和研究人员之间建立信心和信任。因此，所有的参与者都通过带有问卷链接的电子邮件向他们发送了一封附件，详细了解了研究主题及其目的和目标。发送给参与者的所有电子邮件中还附有参与者信息表。参与者自愿参加研究。没有参与这个研究的人员的姓名、年龄、性别、地址等个人问题，这确保了本研究参与者信息的完全保密性。

3.6 Conclusion 结论

To conclude, this research was incorporated using positivist epistemology with deductive approach using quantitative strategy, specifically self-administered questionnaire, as a tool to achieve its aims and objectives. The questionnaire was prepared by using secondary data, which was available through academic literature journals and books. It used non-random sample, specifically convenient sampling technique, to collect data from respondents. During the whole research process and in all stages, it was ensured that confidentiality, ethics, reliability and validity of the research was maintained be referring back again and again to the aims and objectives of the next chapter will present the analysis and critical discussion of the data collected with the academic literature review of the research.

综上所述，本研究采用实证认识论和演绎法相结合的方法，运用定量策略，特别是自编问卷，作为实现研究目的和目标的工具。问卷是利用二手数据编制的，二手数据可通过学术文献期刊和书籍获得。它采用非随机抽样，特别是方便抽样技术，从被调查者那里收集数据。在整个研究过程和各个阶段，确保了研究的保密性、伦理性、可靠性和有效性不断地被重新引用。下一章将结合研究的学术文献综述，对收集的数据进行分析和批判性讨论。

CHAPTER
IV
DATA ANALYSIS AND RESULTS

第四章 / 数据分析和结果

4.1 Introduction 导言

This chapter includes the findings and analysis of the primary research conducted for requirements of an expert witness to be sufficiently independent within forensic accounting. Moreover, it will present the analysis of data through representation of charts, graphs and tables by testing the deduced hypotheses, which are devised in the previous chapter. The data collected from 79 respondents, would be analyzed in IBM SPSS version 20. The results are presented in 3 different sections: demographics, reliability analysis and followed by factor analysis. This chapter will conclude with critical discussion findings with literature review conducted in previous chapters.

本章包括对专家证人在法务会计中充分独立的要求所进行的初步研究的发现和分析。此外，它还将通过对前一章中推导出的假设进行检验，以图表和表格的形式呈现数据分析。把 79 名受访者收集的数据用 IBM SPSS 第（20）版进行分析。研究结果分为三个部分：人口统计学、可靠性分析和因子分析。本章将以批判性的讨论结果和前几章的文献综述得出结论。

4.2 Demographic Analysis 人口统计分析

Demographic analysis is also referred as descriptive statistics in many cases. It is an integral part of research, which provides the description of characteristics of population, and inspection of variables using different statistical techniques（Pallant, 2005）. It summarizes all the collected into numbers in to suitable charts, tables or graphs in a proper format for a reader to understand it quickly. Collecting the responses from target participants through an online questionnaire, was very tough task than it was anticipated. The questionnaire was kept open for 25 days. It was mainly because even after sending 3 reminder emails; there were hardly any number of responses collected from target participants. There could be many reasons for not a prompt response from participants – concerned person on vacations, limited access to Internet due to other important workloads etc. could be anticipated major of them. At few occasions, participants were hesitant to provide information, and they refused to fill the questionnaire. Later on, they were assured about ethical issues and aims and objectives of research in much more detail. However, at the end of 25th day, a total number of 79 respondents filled the online questionnaire. The participants were – Forensic Accountants, Expert Witnesses and Attorneys.

人口统计分析在许多情况下也称为描述性统计。这是研究的一个组成部分，它提供了人口特征的描述，并使用不同的统计技术检验变量（Pallant，2005）。它将收集到的所有数字以适当的格式汇总到适当的图表中以便读者快速理解。通过在线问卷从目标参与者那里收集到的反馈，比预期的要困难得多。问卷开放 25 天。主要是因为即使发了 3 封提醒邮件，几乎没有从

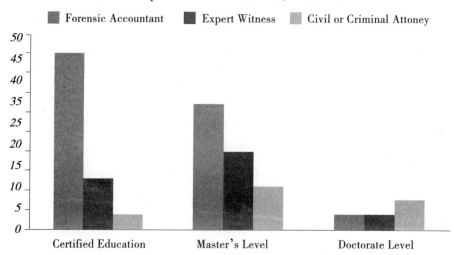

Figure 3 Level of education amongst 79 respondents

表 3 79 名代表者的教育水平

目标参与者那里收集到任何反馈。参与者没有及时做出回复的原因可能有很多，比如度假的相关人员，由于其他重要工作负荷，上网受限等等，这是可预料中的大部分。有几次，参与者不愿提供信息，拒绝填写问卷。后来，他们更详细地了解了伦理问题以及研究的目的和目标。然而，在第25天结束时，共有79名受访者填写了在线问卷，其中包括法务会计师、专家证人和律师。

Figure 3 mentions that out of 79 collected responses, 45 belongs to Forensic Accountants（57%）, 23 belongs to Expert Witnesses（29.1%）and 11 belong to Attorneys（13.9%）. It also shows the level of education amongst respondents. All of them well educated and experienced. Out of 45 forensic accountants, 32 of them are master's level graduated, 4 of them are doctorate while all respondents（45）have certified education（accountants）. Similarly, same pattern could be seen in expert witness as well as in attorneys. Almost all expert witnesses（20 out of 23）are master level educated while 13 of 23 respondents have certification. As expert witnesses should have experience as well as high education level（Matkin, 1983）, it was interesting to find out that only 4 of 23 expert witnesses have doctorate degrees. Criminal or civil attorney respondents have shown a similar pattern as well. All the respondents（11）are master's level educated, 8 of 11 respondents are doctorate in their field while only 4 of total 11 respondents have certified education. Moreover, their doctorate degrees in law cover their certified education requirements.

图3提到，在收集的79份回复中，45份来自法务会计师（57%），23份来自专家证人（29.1%），11份来自律师（13.9%）。它还显示了受访者的教育水平。他们都受过良好的教育，经验丰富。45名司法会计师中，32人硕士毕业，4人博士毕业，45人受过注册教育（会计师）。同样，在专家证人和律师身上也可以看到同样的模式。几乎所有的专家证人（23人中有20人）都受过硕士教育，23名受访者中有13人获得认证。由于专家

证人既要有经验，又要有较高的文化水平（Matkin，1983），令人感兴趣的是，23 名鉴定人中只有 4 人拥有博士学位。刑事或民事律师的回复也表现出类似的模式。所有受访者（11 人）都受过硕士教育，11 名受访者中有 8 人拥有本专业的博士学位，11 名受访者中只有 4 人拥有认证教育。此外，他们的法律博士学位涵盖了他们的认证教育要求。

Professional Experience	No. of Respondents	Doctorate Level	Certified educaqtion	Master's Level
Forensic Accountan	45	4	45	32
0~5 Years	6	0	6	0
11~15Years	22	1	22	20
6~10Years	13	0	13	8
More than 15 Years	4	3	4	4
Expert Witness	23	4	13	20
0~5 Years	3	0	3	0
11~15Years	12	1	7	12
6~10Years	6	1	1	6
More than 15 Years	2	2	2	2
Civil or Criminal Attorney	11	8	4	11
0~5 Years	2	0	0	2
11~15Years	6	6	2	6
6~10Years	1	0	0	1
More than 15 Years	2	2	2	2
职业经验	代表者的数量	博士水平	认证教育	硕士水平
司法会计	45	4	45	32
0~5 年	6	0	6	0
11~15 年	22	1	22	20
6~10 年	13	0	13	8
超过 15 年	4	3	4	4
专家证人	23	4	13	20
0~5 年	3	0	3	0
11~15 年	12	1	7	12
6~10 年	6	1	1	6
超过 15 年	2	2	2	2
民事或刑事诉讼	11	8	4	11
0~5 年	2	0	0	2
11~15 年	6	6	2	6
6~10 年	1	0	0	1
超过 15 年	2	2	2	2

Figure 4　Professional experience of respondents

表格 4　受访者的受教育水平及年限

Figure 4 depicts the professional experience of all respondents with their level of education. More than half (26) of total forensic accountants (45) have more than 10 years of experience. There are only 6 respondents amongst forensic accountants who have up to 5 years of experience while 13 of them have 6–10 years of professional experience. The entire master's level educated forensic accountant falls in the category of more than 5 years of experience while all respondents (4) have more than 15 years of professional experience held a doctorate degree. This is also proven in literature studies done by DiGabriele (2008), where he states that forensic accountants who have extensive experience will have strong academic knowledge as well. All the respondents from the expert witness group have mixed experience as well. There are only 3 respondents who have up to 5 years of experience while major category of respondents fall into 11–15 years of experience (12). There are only 2 respondents, which have more than 15 years of experience but again, both of them hold doctoral degrees; 6 of them have 6–10 years of professional experience. It is interesting to see in expert witness group that all the respondents, irrelevant of their professional experience, holds a master's degree. They are not much into certified education. Nearly 75% (8) of total attorney respondents have more than 10 years of experience and they all hold doctorate degrees. This results indicate that to be an attorney you need to have an enormous amount of experience. All the attorneys are master's level educated irrespective of their professional experience.

图 4 描述了所有受访者的职业经历及其受教育程度。超过半数（26）的司法会计师（45）拥有 10 年以上的工作经验。在法务会计师中，只有 6 名受访者拥有 5 年以上的工作经验，13 名受访者拥有 6~10 年的专业经验。硕士以上学历的法务会计人员全部为 5 年以上经验，被调查者（4 人）具有 15 年以上专业经验，均持有博士学位。DiGabriele（2008）所做的文献研究

中也证明了这一点，他说，经验丰富的法务会计师也将具有很强的学术知识。专家证人组的所有受访者也有不同的经历。只有 3 名受访者有 5 年以上的工作经验，而主要类别的受访者有 11 ~15 年的工作经验（12 年）。仅有 2 名受访者拥有 15 年以上的工作经验，但都拥有博士学位；其中 6 人具有 6 ~10 年的专业经验。有趣的是，在专家证人小组中，所有的被调查者都拥有硕士学位，与他们的专业经历无关。他们不太喜欢认证教育。近 75 %（8）的受访律师拥有 10 年以上的工作经验，都拥有博士学位。这一结果表明，做律师需要有大量的经验。所有的律师都是硕士级别的，不管他们的专业经验如何。

Area of Speciality—Forensic Accountant　Total Respodents=79
擅长领域——法务会计　总共代表人数 =79

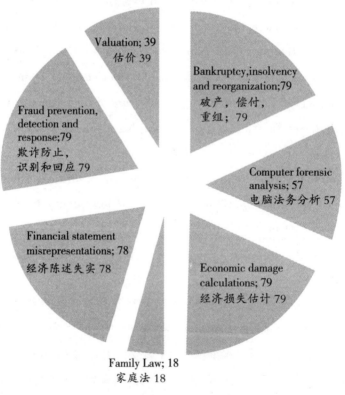

Figure 5: Area of specialty of Forensic Accountant
图 5：法务会计师的专业领域

The question 4 was asked related to the area of specialty for a forensic accountant and for an expert witness specifically. The respondents were given the freedom to answer in multiple choices as well. Figure 5 represents the pie chart only for the area of specialty for a forensic accountant. All the respondents agree that a forensic accountant should have responsibility and area of specialty in fraud calculations and bankruptcy, insolvency and reorganizations. These are very much expected answers from respondents because these all are the areas in which forensic accountants deals with and proved in literature studies as well which is conducted in this research (Crumbley, Heitger, & Smith, 2011; DiGabriele, 2008; Harris & Brown, 2000; Okoye & Akamobi, 2009; Singleton & Singleton, 2010). It was interesting to see that only 57 of total 79 respondents believe that forensic accountant has an area of speciality in forensic computer analysis. According to Singleton & Singleton (2010), the forensic accountant also uses technical and scientific tools to investigate the financial frauds. This research partially agrees with this agreement made by Singleton & Singleton (2010). Half of the respondents consider the valuation disputes as part of the forensic accountant's area of specialty while family law is not considered as a forensic accountant's speciality by a majority of respondents. By scrutinizing the responses received, which is shown in figure 7, it was revealed that nearly 75% (8) of total attorneys and 50% (22) of total forensic accountants respondents consider valuation disputes as an area of specialty of forensic accountants. This would because the respondents who suggested it, would either be working as an expert witness or have worked before within forensic accounting area.

　　问题 4 涉及法务会计师的专业领域，特别是专家证人的专业领域。受访者也有多种选择的自由。图 5 仅表示法务会计师专业领域的饼状图。所有受访者都认为，在欺诈计算、破产、无力偿债和重组方面，法务会计师应该有责任和专长。这些都是非常期待的受访者的回复，因为这些都是法务会计师在本研究中进行的文献研究中处理和证明的领域（Crumbley, Heitger, & Smith, 2011; DiGabriele, 2008; Harris & Brown, 2000; Okoye & Akamobi, 2009; Singleton & Singleton, 2010）。有趣的是，在 79 名受访者中，只有 57 人认为法务会计师具有法证计算机分析的专业领域。据 Singleton &Singleton（2010）介绍，法务会计还利用科技手段对财务欺诈进行调查。本研究部分同意 Singleton 和 Singleton（2010）的协议。半数受访者认为估价纠纷属于法务会计专业领域，而大多数受访者认为家庭法不属于法务会计专业领域。通过仔细查看收到的答复（如图 7 所示），发现近 75 %（8）的律师和 50 %（22）的总法证会计师受访者将估价纠纷视为法务会计师的专业领域。这是因为提出建议的受访者要么是作为专家证人工作，要么是以前在法务

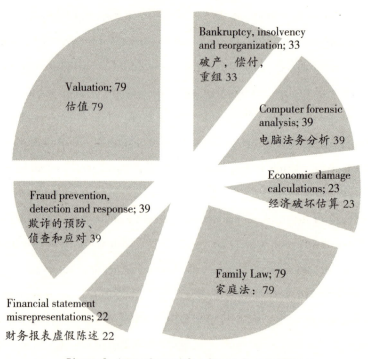

Area of Speciality for an Expert Witness　Total Respodents=79

擅长领域——专家证人　总共代表人数 =79

Figure 6　Area of specialty for an Expert Witness

图 6　专家证人的专业领域

会计领域工作过。

The Figure 6 represents the pie chart for results received from respondents for the area of specialty for an expert witness. All the respondents agree that disputes related to family law and valuation disputes are definitely area of specialty for an expert witness. The other specialty areas like computer forensic analysis, fraud prevention, detection and responses, and bankruptcy, insolvency and reorganizations are partly agreed by respondents regarding area of specialty of an expert witness. By scrutinizing this in more details from figure 7 it was found out that computer forensic analysis, insolvency, bankruptcy and detection and response, reorganization and fraud prevention areas were mostly considered by attorneys and forensic accountants. Nearly 24 respondents from forensic accountants and 7 respondents from attorneys have considered computer forensic analysis as specialty while 22 respondents from forensic accountants and 7 respondents from attorneys have considered fraud prevention, detection and response as specialty. The major reason behind it is because the respondents who suggested this, is still working or would have worked before as an expert witness during testimony. A similar sort of result was obtained is obtained for bankruptcy, insolvency and reorganization where it was very strange to note that the majority of respondents from the expert witness (15) has considered it as their area of specialty. It is assumed that this should be because expert witnesses do deal with these cases in court but they have taken this question as in the general context while other respondents might have seen in corporate and organizational context. The other 2 areas of specialty, namely economic damage calculations and financial misinterpretations, were not considered by a majority of respondents. This is because these are specific areas of auditing accountancy field and a person needs specialized training to do that. However, nearly 10 respondents from forensic accountants group (for both areas) and 6 respondents from attorneys group（for economic damage calculations）have considered it as an area of specialty. This brings forth and approves the findings of Rasmussen & Leauanae（2004）in which he said that professional training is an important aspect for an expert witness in order to succeed within forensic accounting, and the respondents who agreed on the point, must be or would have worked before as an expert witness within forensic accounting.

　　图 6 是专家证人专业领域从受访者那里收到的结果的饼状图。所有受访者都认为，家庭法纠纷和估价纠纷无疑是专家证人的专长领域。其他专业领域，例如电脑法务分析、防止欺诈、侦查和回应以及破产、无力偿债和重整，部分是由受访者就专家证人的专业领域达成协议。通过从图 7 中更详细地研究这一点，发现计算机法务分析、破产、破产和检测与响应、重组和欺诈预防领域主要由律师和司法会计师考虑。近 24 名法务会计师和 7 名律师受访者认为计算机法务分析是专长领域，22 名法务会计师和 7 名律师受访者认为预防、发现和应对欺诈是专长领域。这背后的主要原因是，提出这一建议的受访者仍在工作，或者在作证期间曾作为专家证人工作。在破产、无力偿债和重组方面也取得了类似的结果，令人非常奇怪的是，专家证人（15）的大多数受访者都认为这是他们的专长领域。据认为，这应该是因为专家证人的确在法庭上处理这些案件，但他们把这个问题当作一般情况看待，而其他答卷人可能在公司和组织的情况下看到这个问题。其他两个专业领域，即经济损失计算和财务误解，大多数受访者都没有考虑。这是因为这些都是审计会计领域的具体领域，需要专门培训。然而，近 10 名来自法务会计组（两个领域）的受访者和 6 名来自律师组（经济损失计算）的受访者认为这是一个专业领域。这就提出并认可了 Rasmussen 和 Leauanae （2004）的调查结果，他在调查中说，专业培训是专家证人在法务会计领域取得成功的一个重要方面，同意这一点的被调查者必须是或将会是法务会计领域的专家证人。

	particulars	Forensic Accountants =45	Expert Witness =23	Civil Criminal Attorney=11	Grand Total
Forensic Accountants	Bankruptcy,insolvency and reorganization	45	23	11	79
	Computer forensic analysis	32	17	8	57
	Economic damage calculations	45	23	11	79
	Family Law	10	6	2	18
	Financial statement misrepresentations	44	23	11	78
	Fraud prevention,detection and response	45	23	11	79
	Valuation	22	9	8	39
Forensic Accountants	Bankruptcy,insolvency and reorganization	15	15	3	33
	Computer forensic analysis	24	8	7	39
	Economic damage calculations	10	7	6	23
	Family Law	45	23	11	79
	Financial statement misrepresentations	11	9	2	22
	Fraud prevention,detection and response	22	10	7	39
	Valuation	45	23	11	79

Figure 7   Area of specialty for Forensic Accountants
and an Expert Witness with further detail

	更多细节	法务会计 =45	专家证人 =23	民事/刑事 诉讼 =11	总共
法务会计	破产，无力偿付和重组	45	23	11	79
	电脑法务分析	32	17	8	57
	经济破坏计算	45	23	11	79
	家庭法	10	6	2	18
	财务报表虚假陈述	44	23	11	78
	欺诈的预防、侦查和应对	45	23	11	79
	估价	22	9	8	39

图7   法务会计师和专家证人的专业领域并且答复者提供了更多细节

续表

专家证人	破产，无力偿付和重组	15	15	3	33
	电脑法务分析	24	8	7	39
	经济破坏计算	10	7	6	23
	家庭法	45	23	11	79
	财务报表虚假陈述	11	9	2	22
	欺诈的预防、侦查和应对	22	10	7	39
	估价	45	23	11	79

Furthermore, as mentioned in the previous chapter, respondents were asked about 5 different questions about essential skills, characteristics, competencies of forensic accountants（FA） and expert witnesses（EW）. There was another question asked to respondents regarding requirements for a forensic accountant to be an expert witness. All these questions were asked on Likert scale ranging from "Strongly Disagree to Strongly Agree" and were quantified from 1 to 5, being 1 as strongly disagree and 5 as strongly agree. Figure 8 provides a brief overview of participant's response to these questions with mean and standard deviation.

此外，如前一章所述，受访者被问及 5 个不同的问题，涉及法务会计师（FA）和专家证人（EW）的基本技能、特征、能力。还有一个问题是向受访者提出的，它是关于法务会计师成为专家证人的要求。所有这些问题都是在 Likert 量表上提出的，范围从"强烈不同意"到"强烈同意"，量化范围从 1 到 5，1 表示"强烈不同意"，5 表示"强烈同意"。图 8 简要概述了参与者对这些问题的平均偏差和标准差的反馈。

Factors 因素	Mean 平均值	Std. Deviation Std 偏差
Essential skills FA – Interviewing Skills 法务会计的基本技能 ——面试技巧	4.49	0.766
Essential skills FA – Identification of financial issues 法务会计的基本技能 ——识别财务问题	4.47	0.903

续表

Essential skills FA － Knowledge of Evidence 法务会计的基本技能——证据知识	4.44	0.747
Essential skills FA － Ability to identify frauds with minimal information 法务会计的基本技能——以最少的信息识别欺诈的能力	4.43	0.970
Essential skills FA － Presentation of findings 法务会计的基本技能——展示调查结果	4.35	0.863
Essential skills FA － Knowledge of investigative techniques 法务会计的基本技能——调查技术知识	4.34	0.830
Essential skills FA － Interpretation of financial information 法务会计的基本技能——财务信息解读	4.30	0.965
Essential skills FA － Investigative skills and mentality 法务会计的基本技能——调查技能和心态	4.27	0.983
Essential Competencies FA － Composure 法务会计的基本能力——镇静	4.03	0.947
Essential Competencies FA － Oral and written communication 法务会计的基本能力——口头和书面沟通	3.80	1.137
Essential Competencies FA － Specific legal knowledge 法务会计的基本能力——特定法律知识	3.73	1.227
Essential Competencies FA －Unstructured Problem Solving 法务会计的基本能力——非结构化问题解决	3.67	1.071
Essential Competencies FA －Analytical Proficiency 法务会计的基本能力——分析能力	3.58	1.105
Essential Competencies FA － Investigative flexibility 法务会计的基本能力——调查灵活性	3.51	1.119
Essential Competencies FA － Deductive analysis 法务会计的基本能力——演绎分析	3.35	1.281
Essential Competencies FA － Critical Thinking 法务会计的基本能力——批判性思维	3.15	1.188
Characteristics of FA － Intuitive and Responsive 法务会计的特点——直观、灵敏	4.03	1.250

Characteristics of FA – Generate new ideas and scenarios 法务会计的特点——产生新的想法和场景	3.96	0.967
Characteristics of FA – Adaptive and team player 法务会计的特点——适应并成为队员	3.90	1.081
Characteristics of FA – Detail oriented and insightful 法务会计的特点——面向细节、富有洞察力	3.73	1.071
Characteristics of FA –Make people feel at ease 法务会计的特点——让人感到轻松	3.63	1.242
Characteristics of FA – Analytical and evaluative 法务会计的特点——分析与评价	3.54	1.217
Characteristics of FA – Function well under pressure 法务会计的特点——压力下的功能	3.20	1.213
Characteristics of FA – Skepticism and inquisitive 法务会计的特点——怀疑论与探究	3.18	1.248
Essential Characteristics of EW – Credibility 专家证人的本质特征—— 可信度	4.38	0.938
Essential Characteristics of EW – Ability to formulate an objective opinion 专家证人的本质特征——发表客观意见的能力	4.37	0.819
Essential Characteristics of EW – Ability to provide consistent testimony 专家证人的基本特征——提供一致证词的能力	4.24	0.923
Essential Characteristics of EW – Knowledge, education, and training 专家证人 W 的本质特征——知识、教育和训练	4.14	0.971
Essential Characteristics of EW – Experience 专家证人的本质特征——经验	4.08	1.071
Essential Characteristics of EW – Investigative orientation 专家证人的本质特征——调查取向	3.97	1.281
Essential Skills of EW – Reasoning skills and abilities 专家证人的基本技术——推理能力	4.24	0.950
Essential Skills of EW – Ability to persuade others 专家证人的基本技能——说服他人的能力	4.19	1.156

续表

Essential Skills of EW - Teaching and writing abilities 专家证人的基本技能——教学与写作能力	4.15	0.935
Essential Skills of EW - Inquisitive skills 专家证人的基本技能——好奇技能	4.13	0.979
Essential Skills of EW - Mediagenic abilities 专家证人的基本技能——媒体能力	4.04	1.068
Essential Skills of EW - Public speaking ability 专家证人的基本技能——演讲能力	4.03	1.074
Essential Skills of EW - Prior experience 专家证人的基本技能——以往经验	3.92	1.248
Essential Skills of EW - Analytical ability 专家证人的基本技能——分析能力	3.91	1.303
Requirements for FA to be an EW- Skeptic and diplomat 司法会计成为一个专家证人的要求——怀疑论者和外交家	4.43	0.763
Requirements for FA to be an EW- Extensive experience 司法会计成为一个专家证人的要求——广泛的经验	4.32	0.927
Requirements for FA to be an EW- Academic qualifications 司法会计成为专家证人的要求——学术资历	4.24	0.923
Requirements for FA to be an EW- Teaching abilities 司法会计成为专家证人的要求——教学能力	4.06	1.274
Requirements for FA to be an EW- Excellent communication skills 司法会计成为专家证人的要求——优秀的沟通能力	3.96	1.305
Requirements for FA to be an EW- Professional training 司法会计成为专家证人的要求——专业的训练	3.90	1.093

Figure 8 Mean statistics for characteristics, skills, competencies of FA and EW
图 8 FA 和 EW 的特征、技能、能力的平均统计

As it can be seen from the figure, the majority of respondents agree with most of the skills, characteristics, competencies required to be a successful forensic accountant and an expert witness. For forensic accountants, the identified skills asked in question include investigative skills in accounting (ability to identify frauds with minimal information − 4.43 mean; identification of financial issues − 4.47 mean) which has shown high mean and considered being one of the topmost skills to be in forensic accounting. Similarly, the high means in oral and written communication (3.80) and specific legal knowledge (3.73) amongst the competencies shows that these are most important requirements in forensic accountant. However, critical thinking and deductive analysis, with a mean of 3.15 and 3.35 respectively, has been considered as least important competencies in forensic accountants. Intuitive and responsive (4.03) and generating new business ideas (3.96) are considered to be topmost characteristics in forensic accountants along with analytical and evaluative abilities (3.54) . It was quite interesting that skepticism and inquisitive (3.18) were considered least important in this sample which contradicts the findings suggested by DiGabriele (2008) . Reasoning skills and abilities (4.24) , communication skills (4.03) and analytical skills (3.91) have been considered has topmost skills set required in expert witnesses. Furthermore, all the characteristics for an expert witness mentioned in the questionnaire were also considered being most important ones, which are essentially required in them. Similarly, the requirements for the forensic accountant to be an effective expert witness were also agreed by respondents to be essentially present in them. This supports the findings of DiGabriele (2008) and Rasmussen & Leauanae (2004) which mentions extensive experience, professional training and academic qualifications are the important requirements for any forensic accountant to be successful as an expert witness.

　　从图中可以看出，大部分受访者都认同成为一名成功的法务会计师和专家证人所需的大部分技能、特点和能力。对于法务会计师，所询问的鉴定技能包括会计调查技能（用最少信息鉴定欺诈的能力 –4.43 均值；财务问题的识别 –4.47 均值），它显示出很高的均值，被认为是法务会计中最重要的技能之一。同样，能力中口头和书面交流的高手段（3.80）和具体的法律知识（3.73）表明，这些是法务会计最重要的要求。然而，批判性思维和演绎分析，平均分别为 3.15 和 3.35，被认为是法务会计师最不重要的能力。直觉和反应（4.03）以及产生新的商业想法（3.96）被认为是法务会计师最重要的特征，还有分析和评估能力（3.54）。有趣的是，怀疑和好奇（3.18）在这个样本中被认为是最不重要的，这与 DiGabriele（2008）提出的发现相矛盾。推理技能和能力（4.24）、沟通技能（4.03）和分析技能（3.91）被认为是鉴定人所需要的最高技能。此外，问卷中提到的专家证人的所有特征也被认为是最重要的特征，这些特征在问卷中基本上是必需的。同样，答卷人也同意法务会计师必须是有效的专家证人的要求，认为他们基本上在场。这支持了 DiGabriele（2008）与 Rasmussen & Leauanae（2004）的调查结果，其中提到广泛的经验、专业培训和学术资格是任何法务会计师作为专家证人取得成功的重要条件。

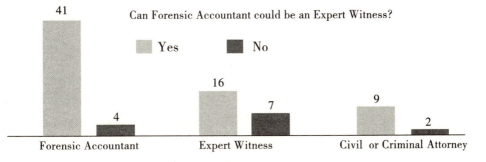

Figure 9　Forensic Accountant being an Expert Witness

图 9　法务会计师是专家证人

Lastly, it was asked from respondents about whether they ever played the role of expert witness or not. 40 respondents said they never played the role of while 39 have played the role of an expert witness. Out of 39 respondents, 16 were forensic accountants and 23 were expert witnesses. It was also asked to respondents about their opinion on forensic accountants being an expert witness. The results are described in figure 9 above.

最后，被调查者询问他们是否曾经扮演过专家证人的角色。40 名受访者表示，他们从未扮演过专家证人的角色，39 名受访者则扮演过专家证人的角色。在 39 名受访者中，16 人是法务会计师，23 人是专家证人。还向受访者询问了他们对法务会计师作为专家证人的看法。图 9 中描述这一结果。

4.3 Reliability Analysis 可靠性分析

Prior to understanding the inferential analysis of the data for testing the hypotheses devised the internal consistency of factors and variables needs to be measured. This should be done by running through reliability analysis. It indicates how much data is free from random error. According to Bryman and Bell（2007）, most researchers use Cronbach's alpha coefficient to check the reliability of data. The values of Cronbach's alpha are highly sensitive and their value should be $1 > \alpha > 0.7$（Pallant, 2005）. The results are mentioned in Figure 10 below:

在理解用于测试假设的数据推断分析之前，需要测量因素和变量的内部一致性。这应该通过可靠性分析来完成。它表示有多少数据没有随机误差。据 Bryman 和 Bell（2007）介绍，大多数研究人员使用克朗巴赫的 alpha 系数来检验数据的可靠性。Cronbach 的 alpha 值是高度敏感的，它们的值应该是 $1 > \alpha > 0.7$（Pallant，2005）。结果如图 10 所示。

Scale	Cranbach's Alpha	No.of items
Essential Skills for Forensic Accountant		
Essential Competences of Forensic Accountant		
Essential Traits and Characteristics of Forensic Accountant		
Essential Skills and Abilities for an Expert Witness		
Essential Characteristics for an Expert Witness		
EssentialRequirements for Forensic Accountant to be an Expert Witness		

Figure 10 Reliability Analysis

规模	各自变量	项目个数
法务会计师的基本技能	0.68	8
法务会计师的基本能力	0.586	8
法务会计师的基本特征和特点	0.413	8
专家证人的基本特征和技能	0.425	8
专家证人的基本特征	0.595	8
法务会计师变成专家证人的基本要求	0.756	8

图 10 可靠性分析

According to DeVillis (2003), Cronbach's alpha coefficient should be above 0.7. However, whenever your numbers of items are low or less than 10 items, then Briggs and Cheek (1986) suggested that the optimal range for internal consistency should be 0.4 and should be taken as just enough. As it can be seen that essential skills for forensic accountants (0.68) and essential requirements for a forensic accountant to be an expert witness (0.756) shows relatively high internal consistency among their own variables. However, according to Pallant (2005), essential competencies of a forensic accountant (0.586) and essential characteristics for an expert witness (0.595) also show just enough internal consistency among their own factors. The other factors could be taken as just enough as well because as there are less of variables among all factors（DeVillis, 2003）- essential traits and characteristics of a forensic accountant（0.413）and essential skills and abilities of an expert witness（0.425）.

根据 DeVillis（2003），克朗巴赫的 alpha 系数应该在 0.7 以上。然而，每当你的项目数量少于 10 个时，Briggs 和 Cheek（1986）建议内部一致性的最佳范围应该是 0.4，并且应该被认为是足够的。可以看出，法务会计师的基本技能（0.68）和法务会计师成为专家证人的基本要求（0.756）在各自变量之间表现出相对较高的内在一致性。然而，据 Pallant（2005）说，法务会计师的基本能力（0.586）和专家证人的基本特征（0.595）也显示了他们自身因素之间的足够的内在一致性。其他因素也同样可以考虑，因为在所有因素中变量较少（DeVillis，2003）——法务会计的基本特征和特点（0.413）和专家证人的基本技能和能力（0.425）。

4.4 Factor Analysis 因子分析

Factor analysis is a statistical technique through which the large data dispersed among different factors can be reduced or summarized its different tests and thus thereby giving you a smaller set of more relevant factors or components（Pallant, 2005）. For the purpose of this research, there were 3 different factor analysis were run on SPSS with regards to essential skills, traits and characteristics and competencies of forensic accountants（24 different factors）, skills and characteristics of an expert witness（14 different factors）and essential requirements for a forensic accountant to be self-sufficient in expert witness field. Before performing principal component analysis（PCA）to these factors, there should be an assessment for these factors whether they are good enough to go through factor analysis or not. Therefore, for this purpose, Kaiser-Meyer-Oklin（KMO）and Barlett's Test of Sphericity should be run through

SPSS（Pallant, 2005）. According to Pallant（2005）, the KMO value should be more than 0.6 and should reach supporting the factorability of the correlation matrix with Chi-Square statistics（Pallant, 2005）. The results are shown in below figure 11.

因子分析是一种统计技术，通过它可以减少或总结分散在不同因素中的大量数据的不同测试，从而给你一组更相关的因子或成分（Pallant, 2005）。本研究在 SPSS 上对法务会计人员的基本技能、特点和能力（24 个不同因素）、专家证人的技能和特点（14 个不同因素）以及法务会计人员在专家证人领域自给自足的基本要求进行了 3 个不同的因素分析。在对这些因素进行主成分分析（PCA）之前，应该对这些因素进行评估，看它们是否足以进行因子分析。为此，Kaiser – Meyer – Oklin（KMO）和 Barlett 的球形度测试应通过 SPSS 进行（Pallant, 2005）。根据 Pallant（2005），KMO 值应该大于 0.6，并且应该达到用卡方统计来支持相关矩阵的可因子性（Pallant, 2005）。结果如图 11 所示。

统计量检验和巴特利球检验			
	对法务会计	对专家证人	对二者
取样足够的 Kaiser – M – O 度量	562	608	784
巴列特球度检验约卡方	510.280	192.297	101.093
	276	91	15
	000	000	000

Figure 11 KM and Bartlett's test for sampling adequacy
图 11 KM 和 Bartlett 的抽样充足性测试

The value for KMO and Bartlett's test for 24 different factors forensic accountants is just below 0.6（0.562）and Chi-square is also significantly sufficient at 510.280. This does not support the arguments by Pallant（2005）but however it could be taken for educational research purposes as the sample size is not large enough to prove that DeVillis（2003）. Thus, the principal component analysis was performed with varimax rotation. This in the end revealed the presence of 8 components with Eigen values more than 1 for a forensic accountant factors（refer to Appendix B）, 6 components with Eigen values than 1 for expert witness（refer to Appendix B）and only 1 component with Eigen values more than 1 for the requirement for a forensic accountant to be an expert witness（refer to Appendix B）.

KMO 和 Bartlett 对 24 个不同因素的法务会计师的测试值略低于 0.6（0.562），卡方也在 510.280 显著足够。这并不支持 Pallant（2005）的论点，但是它可以用于教育研究目的，因为样本量不足以证明 DeVillis（2003）。因此，主成分分析是用 varimax 旋转进行的。这最终揭示了法务会计要素特征值大于 1 的 8 个分量（参见附录 B），鉴定人特征值大于 1 的 6 个分量（参见附录 B），鉴定人成为鉴定人的要求只有特征值大于 1 的 1 个分量（参见附录 B）。

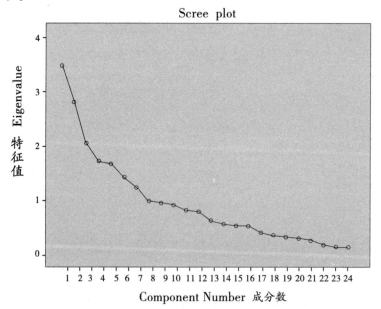

Figure 12 Scree plot for forensic accountants
图 12　法务会计师的 Scree 图

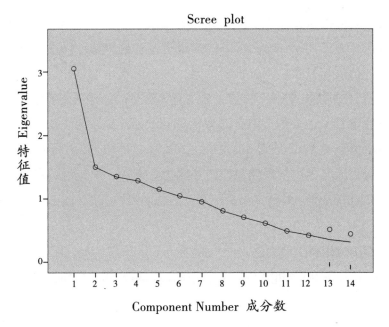

Figure 13 Scree plot for expert witnesses
图 13　专家证人的 Scree 图

Using Cattell's scree (Pallant, 2005) test, the result were still unclear and required the need for the Parallel analysis. When it was implemented with varimax rotation, it provided much clearer picture of the factors to be taken into consideration and factors with Eigen values exceeding the corresponding Eigen values generated by analysis the same size of 24 variables for forensic accountants and 14 variables for expert witness. This research will not take in to consideration for the requirement for a forensic accountant to be an expert witness as it just showed 1 component to be extracted, and for principal component analysis there should be at least 10 factors (Pallant, 2005) . Initially it was considered so as to check whether it is worthwhile considering it for academic purposes but looking at results, it is decided not to take into consideration. Therefore, it has been decided to go with 8 different factors for a forensic accountant and 6 different factors for expert witnesses.

使用 Cattell 的 scree（Pallant，2005）测试，结果仍然不清楚，需要进行平行分析。在使用 varimax rotation 实现时，它更清楚地描述了要考虑的因素以及特征值超过相应特征值的因素，这些因素是通过分析相同大小的 24 个法务会计师变量和 14 个专家证人变量而产生的。这项研究将不考虑法务会计师作为专家证人的要求，因为它只显示了要提取的一个成分，主成分分析至少应该有 10 个因素（Pallant，2005）。最初是为了检查是否值得为了学术目的而考虑，但看结果决定不考虑。因此，决定对一名法务会计适用 8 个不同的因素，对鉴定人适用 6 个不同的因素。

4.5 Discussion 讨论

After running through different statistical tools and factor analysis, the factors, which are derived from, the results of principal component analysis which have shown greater degree of reliability and more confidence in results are as follows:

经过不同的统计工具和因子分析，从主成分分析的结果中得出的因子表现出更高的可靠性并对结果更加确信，这些因子如下：

For Forensic Accountants:

法务会计师：

· Critical Thinking as essential competencies in forensic accountant;

批判性思维是法务会计的基本能力；

· Unstructured Problem Solving Thinking as essential competencies in forensic accountant;

非结构化问题解决思维是法务会计的基本能力；

· Knowledge of evidence as essential characteristics of a forensic accountant;

证据知识是法务会计师的基本特征；

· Skepticism and inquisitiveness as essential characteristics of a forensic accountant;

怀疑和好奇是法务会计师的基本特征；

· Intuitive and responsive as essential characteristics of a forensic accountant;

直觉和反应灵敏使法务会计的基本特征；

· Oral and written communication skills as essential competencies for a forensic accountant;

口头和书面沟通技能是法务会计师的基本能力；

· Analytical Proficiency as essential competencies for a forensic accountant;

分析能力是法务会计师的基本能力；

· Specific legal knowledge as essential competencies for a forensic accountant.

法律专业知识是法务会计的基本能力。

For Expert Witnesses:

对于专家证人：

· Experience as essential characteristics of an expert witness;

经验作为专家证人的基本特征；

· Credibility as essential characteristics of an expert witness;

可信度作为专家证人的基本特征；

· Public speaking ability as essential skills for an expert witness;

演讲能力是专家证人的基本技能；

· Prior experience as essential skills for an expert witness;

以往经验是专家证人的基本技能；

· Ability to persuade others as essential skills for an expert witness;

说服他人成为专家证人的基本技能的能力；

· Knowledge, education, and training as essential skills for an expert witness.

知识、教育和培训是专家证人的基本技能。

Also, the results which we have seen from the mean of different factors and requirements related for a forensic accountant to be self-sufficient in expert witness field suggest all of them are agreeable to respondents as the mean of all 6 factors was above 6. Therefore on this behalf, this research will take its hypotheses one by one and will critically discuss with literature.

此外，从不同因子和要求的均值来看，法务会计师在专家证人领域自给自足的结果表明，所有这些因素都是被调查者所认同的，因为所有6个因素的均值都在6以上。为此，本研究将逐一提出假设，并与文献进行批判性讨论。

H1-Forensic Accountant in expert witnessing should have extensive experience, be professionally trained and high academic qualifications as its characteristics.

H1—法务会计师作为专家证人，应具有丰富的经验，经过专业培训，具有较高的学历。

As the results suggest in requirements in forensic accountant to be an expert witness, the mean for extensive experience was 4.32, professionally trained was 3.90 and academic qualifications was 4.24. This suggests a high degree of agreeableness amongst respondents. This was also mentioned in various studies conducted by DiGabriele（2008）, Okoye & Akamobi（2009）and Rasmussen & Leauanae（2004）. This could be seen in results seen after factor analysis of essential skills, traits and characteristics and competencies for forensic accountants and expert witness respectively. The factor analysis of forensic accountants shows specific legal knowledge while the factor analysis of expert witnesses shows knowledge, education, and training as essential skills for an expert witness. This supports the argument made by Bronstein（1999）, Feder（1991）, Iyer（1993）, Poynter（1997）, Wilkerson（1997）, Matson（1999） and Weikel & Hughes（1993）. All these scholars have suggested that in order to be a successful expert witness, an individual must have knowledge, education, training and extensive experience in their filed so that they can stand against the opposing party in trial testimony in the courtrooms. This would also help the judges and the jury members to understand and resolve the issues which have complex in nature Poynter（1997）. Therefore, on this behalf, this hypotheses is accepted.

结果显示，法务会计师成为专家证人的要求是：丰富的经验平均为 4.32 人，受过专业培训的为 3.90 人，学历为 4.24 人。这表明受访者的亲和力很高。DiGabriele（2008）、Okoye & Akamobi（2009）以及 Rasmussen & Leauanae（2004）进行的各种研究也提到了这一点。这可以从对法务会计师和专家证人的基本技能、特点和能力分别进行因素分析后得出的结果中看出。法务会计师的因素分析显示了特定的法律知识，而专家证人的因素分析显示知识、教育和培训是专家证人的基本技能这些都支持 Bronstein（1999）、Feder（1991）、Iyer（1993）、Poynter（1997）、Wiklkerson（1997）、Matson（1999）与 Weikel 和 Hughs（1993）的论点。所有这些学者都认为，一个人要成为一名成功的专家证人，必须具备相关的知识、教育、培训和丰富的经验，才能在出庭作证时与对方对抗。这也将有助于法官和陪审团成员理解和解决性质复杂的 Poynter（1997）问题。因此，在这方面，这个假设是可以接受的。

H2 - Forensic Accountant should have diplomat skills and excellent communication skills to be an expert witness.

H2——法务会计师应具备外交技巧和良好的沟通技巧，才能成为专家证人。

The results in requirements for a forensic accountant to be successful expert witness for excellent communication skills suggest agreeableness to the factor by mean of 3.96 of 79 respondents. The same was noted with a mean of 4.43 for skepticism and diplomat skills as well. This hypothesis was derived from the studies conducted by DiGabriele（2008）, Rasmussen & Leauanae（2004）, Okoye & Akamobi（2009）, Faherty（1995）, Feder（1991）and Messmer（2004）. They all have suggested that interpersonal and communication skills aids in disseminating information about the company's ethics and information collected as evidences to support testimony in the courtroom. Also, this would be of great advantage for a forensic accountant working as an expert witness because they also have an understanding of criminal and civil law, the legal system, court procedures, accounting auditing and skeptic attitude（DiGabriele, 2008）. This skills aid to the forensic accountants in dealing the case professionally and present their case strongly in the courtrooms against frauds committed. Poytner（1997）have stated that expert witness in forensic accountant should be always be a diplomat and political in order to resolve the cases. This is because they should be independent of the parties to the dispute and be able to demonstrate proof of interpretations made by them on the basis of assumed facts. This was also made relevant in studies conducted by Singleton & Singleton, 2010）and Iyer（1993）. Therefore, on this ground and the results received from respondents, the hypothesis is accepted.

在 79 名受访者中，有 3.96 人的调查结果显示，要求法务会计师成为具备优秀沟通技巧的成功专家证人，符合这一因素。怀疑论者和外交家的技巧也以 4.43 分的平均值被注意到。这一假设源自 DiGabriele（2008）、Rasmussen 和 Leauanae（2004）、Okoye 和 Akamobi（2009）、Faherty（1995）、Feder（1991）和 Messmer（2004）进行的研究。他们都表示，人际交往和沟通技巧有助于传播有关公司道德的信息和收集的信息，作为出庭作证的证据。此外，这对于作为专家证人的法务会计师来说也是非常有利的，因为他们也了解刑法和民法、法律制度、法庭程序、会计审计和怀疑态度（DiGabriele, 2008）。这一技能有助于法务会计专业处理案件，并在法庭上有力地陈述案情，以打击欺诈行为。Poytner（1997）指出，法务会计专家证人应该始终是外交官和政治人士，才能解决案件。这是因为他们应该独立于争端各方，能够证明他们根据假定事实所作的解释。这一点与 Singleton & Singleton, 2010）和 Iyer（1993）进行的研究相关。因此，基于这一点，从受访者那里得到的结果，这个假设是可以接受的。

H3 - Forensic accountant should possess skeptic, investigative and analytical abilities as its competencies to be able to self-sufficient in expert witnessing.

H3—法务会计师应具备怀疑、调查和分析作为其能力使其能够成为自立的专家证人。

The results in this all these factors findings were quite interesting to see amongst the various factors those are mentioned in skills, characteristics and competencies of forensic accountants and expert witnesses. Although this was excepted in the responses for requirements for forensic accountants to be an expert witness with a mean of 4.43 but it was partially accepted in skills, characteristics and competencies of forensic accountants and expert witnesses related to investigative, analytical skills and skepticism. They all were more or less just above to neutral category. This could be because of the smaller sample size. However, the studies conducted by DiGabriele（2008）, Okoye & Akamobi（2009）, Faherty（1995）, Feder（1991）and Messmer（2004）have shown that these are important exhibits for any forensic accountant to be successful as an expert witness. In fact, Poytner（1997）and Bronstein（1999）have shown one of the foremost important skill to be needed for a forensic accountant to be successful as an expert witness. This could also be rejected on the ground because as an expert witness, itself, is a different field from forensic accounting, they can deal with the cases more effectively. All they have to show and understand the subject in a deeper level so that they can make it understand to judge and the jury members in case, if the testimony is too much complicated. This is being shown in Feder（1991）Iyer（1993）Wilkerson（1997）, Matson（1999）and Weikel & Hughes（1997）as an expert witness has to show their abilities before appearing for testimony. So this could be partially accepted in this research. Further research in this area is recommended.

所有这些因素的结果在法务会计师和专家证人的技能、特征和能力中提到的各种因素中是相当有趣的。虽然这一点在要求法务会计师成为平均4.43人的专家证人的答复中被排除在外，但在法务会计师和专家证人有关调查、分析技能和质疑的技能、特点和能力方面，这一点部分被接受。他们都或多或少地略高于中性类别。这可能是因为样本量较小。然而，DiGabriele（2008）、Okoye 和 Akamobi（2009）、Faherty（1995）、Feder（1991）和 Messmer（2004）进行的研究表明，这些都是任何一名法务会计作为专家证人取得成功的重要证据。事实上，Poytner （1997）和 Bronstein （1999）已经证明了法务会计师作为专家证人取得成功所需要的最重要的技能之一。这也可以被驳回，因为作为一名专家证人，本身与法务会计是不同的领域，他们可以更有效地处理案件。如果证词过于复杂，他们所需要的只是更深层次的展示和理解，以便让法官和陪审团成员在案件中理解。这一点在 Feder（1991）、Iyer（1993）、Wiklkerson（1997）、Matson（1999） 和 Weikel & Hughes（1997）都有所体现，因为专家证人在出庭作证前必须展示自己的能力。所以这在本研究中可以部分接受并建议在这方面进一步研究。

4.6 Conclusion 结论

In summary, this chapter provided with a brief analysis of data collected from 79 respondents. Using SPSS 20, the hypotheses, which were deduced from the literature review, were being tested with different statistical analysis and tools and descriptive analysis. The factor analysis has deduced 8 major factors for a forensic accountant skills, characteristics and competencies while

6 different major factors for expert witness skill and characteristics. Based on this H1 and H2 were fully accepted while H3 was kind of partially accepted due to insignificant number of respondents. This is one of the major reasons for its partial acceptance. A further discussion with findings and literature is revealed relation of hypotheses tested with theory. The next chapter will focus on the conclusion and recommendations for further research.

综上所述，本章简要分析了从 79 名受访者中获得的数据。使用 SPSS 20，对文献综述中推导出的假设进行了不同的统计分析以及描述性分析。因子分析得出了影响法务会计技能、特征和能力的 8 个主要因素，而影响专家证人技能和特征的 6 个主要因素。在此基础上，H1 和 H2 被完全接受，而 H3 由于被调查者人数不多而被部分接受。这是部分接受的主要原因之一。在前人研究成果和文献基础上的进一步讨论揭示了用理论来检验假设的关系。下一章将着重于结论和对进一步研究提出建议。

CHAPTER
V

CONCLUSION,
LIMITATIONS, AND
IMPLICATIONS

第五章 / 结论、局限
和规范

5.1 Conclusion 结论

This paper sought to answer the research question: what the major requirements for an expert witness to be self-sufficient within forensic accounting. The deep literature review was conducted to provide a microscopic lens with which to go into deeper insights into the forensic accounting profession and expert witnesses and their characteristics, skills, knowledge and competencies. The various studies conducted by scholars gave a deeper and denser insight to the subject specifically by DiGabriele (2008), Rasmussen & Leauanae (2004) and Poytner (1997) as their work were more related to the field on which the research is fundamentally based. However, although it was relatively straightforward to identify the skill sets for both individually and then presenting it in the research report by taking common in between them. But there are some specific issues, which can be dealt only by forensic accountants as their field is more of investigative, analytical and skeptic nature, which calls for the research to be conducted. This study has identified substantial disparity within the respondents who belong to industry with regard to skills, characteristics and competencies of forensic accountants and expert witnesses. There were 79 respondents with a plethora of qualifications, skills, certifications and experience amongst the respondents analyzed. However, they differ on their view on the individual skill sets of forensic accountants and expert witnesses but they were pretty much agreeable on standard skill set for a forensic accountant as an expert witness in their responses. Therefore, the 3 hypotheses devised, 2 of they were fully accepted while 1 of them was partially accepted due to insignificant number in the sample.

本文试图回答这样一个研究问题：在法务会计师中，成为专家证人的主要要求是什么。深入的文献综述为深入了解法务会计专业和专家证人及其特点、技能、知识和能力提供了微观视角。学者们所做的各种研究，特别是DiGabriele（2008）、Rasmussen & Leauanae（2004）和 Poytner（1997）的研究，对这一课题有了更深入和更深刻的了解，因为他们的工作与研究的根本基础领域更相关。然而，虽然比较简单的是，单独确定两个人的技能组合，然后通过他们之间的共同点在研究报告中呈现出来，但也有一些具体的问题，只有法务会计师才能解决，因为他们的领域更多的是调查性、分析性和怀疑性，需要进行研究。这项研究发现，在法务会计师和专家证人的技能、特点和能力方面，业内受访者之间存在很大差距。在被分析的受访者中，有 79 人拥有资质、技能、认证和经验。不过，他们对法务会计师和鉴定人的个人技能有不同的看法，但对法务会计师作为专家证人的标准技能却相当认同。因此，设计的 3 个假设中，有 2 个被完全接受，1 个由于样本数量不多而被部分接受。

5.2 Implications 影响

This research has contributed towards theory and practice. In theory, the research has revisited the skills of forensic accountants and expert witnesses and helped in examining them from a professional point of view. In practice, it will help for those who would like to make their career within forensic accounting and provides the ground work for those who want to do more research in this topic. As the analysis has shown that the skills, characteristics and competencies of forensic accountants and expert witnesses, the highlights of the fact is that it shows the important skill set required to be sufficiently independent within both fields individually as well as simultaneously. Few of the highlights in choosing a forensic accountant as an expert witness are as follows.

　　这项研究有助于理论和实践的发展。理论上，这项研究重新审视了法务会计师和专家证人的技能，并帮助他们从专业的角度进行检查。在实践中，这将有助于那些想在法务会计领域里获得较高地位的人，也为那些想在这方面做更多研究的人提供基础工作。由于分析显示，法务会计师和鉴定人的技能、特点和能力，突出的事实是，它显示了在两个领域中单独和同时充分独立所需的重要技能。选择法务会计师作为专家证人的重点很少。

　　· For a forensic accountant to be an expert witness he/she should be a qualified expert in the field of forensic accounting and most likely experienced and accredited from well know insitutions in the filed.

　　法务会计师要成为专家证人，他 / 她应该是法务会计领域的合格专家，最有可能是经验丰富并获得该领域知名机构的认证。

　　· The expert witness in the respective case should have no personal, proffessional or legal relation to any of the parties involved avoiding conflict of interest in the case.

　　各自案件中的专家证人应与任何相关方没有个人、专业或法律关系以避免案件中的利益冲突。

　　· The expert witness should be up-to-date with the current research. Though there is no exact way of testing this point renewal of certification or membership with proffessional institutions can be taken as an indication of the same.

　　专家证人应了解当前研究的最新情况。尽管没有确切的方法来检验这一点，但是专业机构的认证或会员资格的更新可以被看作是一种暗示。

　　· The expert witness in the respective case should be able to provide the justification for opinion provided so as to ensure that the provided witness withstands the cross examinations and be credible.

　　各自案件中的专家证人应能够为所提供的意见提供理由，以确保所提供的证人经得起盘问并具有可信度。

Finally, potential seeds for future research can be perceived. As this research has attempted to find requirements of an expert witness to be self-sufficient within forensic accounting, which was limited due to small sample size of only 79 respondents, it is recommended to do, furthermore, deeper and denser research in this area. A larger sample and qualitative analysis is recommended for further research. The advantage of a qualitative approach is more evident as quantitative nature will make some different perception while reading or filling out questionnaire. The qualitative analysis makes much more clearly the research's aims and objective. Therefore, conducting a qualitative research is recommended and it will give more insight about requirements for an expert witness to be self-sufficient within forensic accounting.

最后，可以看到未来研究的潜在种子。由于这项研究试图在法务会计中找到成为专家证人的要求，但由于只有79名受访者样本较少，因此受到限制，因此建议在这一领域进行更深入、更密集的研究。建议进一步研究更多的样本和定性分析。定性方法的优势更加明显，因为定量性质在阅读或填写问卷时会产生一些不同的感觉。定性分析更加明确了研究的目标和任务。因此，建议进行定性研究，这样可以更深入地了解在法务会计方面成为专家证人的要求。

5.3 Research Limitations 研究局限

One of the main highlights of this study is the lack of existing literature on Forensic accounting and expert witness in UK context. Due to this gap in literature the foundation of this study was mainly based on literature review in the US. There are differences in the law of US and UK and hence for this study this is the most important limitation. Given the limited time available to complete such a wider area of research topic, the clear aims, objectives and purpose to have strong primary research led the self-administered questionnaire to be designed very simplistically and specifically. However, there were still a number of issues confronted in gathering data for research. Firstly, as due to time constraints, participants were contacted by sending an online link for questionnaire in e-mails. The contact information was taken out from different websites of association of forensic accountants, association of expert witness and London solicitor litigation association. All websites contains member's information like their contact numbers, address etc. but only few of them make it available to common people, in which case the questionnaire were sent to the companies which in most cases did not respond. Hence with around 400 participants were selected to send an online link of questionnaire and only 79 responses were recorded successfully and in proper way to be used for analysis. Secondly, although a very conscious effort was made to contact the right person in the organization to fill the survey, but in a large organization it was very hard to get hold of the right person. Therefore, responses from those organizations, which a researcher was not sure about validity, have been removed. This has also made a significant amount of responses to be collected.

　　这项研究的主要亮点之一是缺乏英国背景下的法务会计和专家证人方面的现有文献。由于这一文献空白，本研究的基础主要是基于美国的文献综述。美国和英国的法律有所不同，因此对这项研究来说，这是最重要的限制。鉴于完成如此广泛的研究课题的时间有限，进行强有力的初步研究的明确的目标、任务和目的导致自行设计的问卷非常简单和具体。然而，在收集数据进行研究方面仍然面临一些问题。首先，由于时间限制，参与者通过发送电子邮件中的问卷在线链接进行联系。联系方式取自法务会计师协会、专家证人协会和伦敦律师诉讼协会的不同网站。所有网站都包含会员的联系电话、地址等信息。但只有很少一部分提供给普通人，在这种情况下，问卷被发送给大多数情况下没有回复的公司。因此，大约400名参与者被选中发送一个在线问卷链接，只有79份回复被成功记录下来，并以适当的方式用于分析。其次，虽然很有意识地努力联系组织中合适的人来填写调查，但是在一个大的组织中很难找到合适的人。因此，研究人员对这些组织的反应并不确定是否有效，这些反应已经被删除。这也就需要我们收集大量的答复。

Bibliography 参考文献

[1]Aderibigbe, P. The Role of the Forensic Chartered Accountant [J]. *In Nigeria Accountant*, 2000, July.

[2] Appelbaum, P. The ethics of expert testimony in an advocate's world [J]. *Bulletin of the American Academy of Psychiatry and the Law*, 1987, 15 (1): 15-25.

[3] Bologna, J. G., & Lindquist, R. J. *Fraud auditing and forensic accounting* [M]. New York: Wiley, 1995.

[4] Bridger, D. Specializing in litigation support services[J]. *International Financial Law Review*,1992, August: 5-8.

[5] Briggs, S. R., & Cheek, J. M. The role of factor analysis in the development and evaluation of personality scales[J]. *Journal of Personality*,1986,54 (1):106-148.

[6] Bronstein, D.*Law for the expert witness* [M]. Boca Raton, FL: CRC Press,1999.

[7] Bryman, A., & Bell, E. *Business Research Methods* (3rd ed.)[M]. New York: Oxford University Press,2011.

[8] Buckhoff, T. A. & J.D. Hansen. Interviewing as a "Forensic-type" Procedure[J]. *Journal of Forensic Accounting*, 2002, 3(1): 1-16.

[9] Buckhoff, T.A. Cash: The favorite target of fraudsters[J]. *CPA Journal*, 2004, 7: 63.

[10] Buckoff, T. A., & Schrader, R. A. The teaching of forensic accounting in the United States[J].*Journal of Forensic Accounting*, 2000,1:135–146.

[11] Carmines, E., & R. Zeller. *Reliability and Validity Assessment*[M]. Newbury Park, CA: Sage, 1979.

[12] Casey, P. Expert testimony in court: General Principles[J]. *Advances in Psychiatric Treatment*. 2003, vol. 9.

[13] Christensen, J., Byington, J.R., & T.J. Blalock.Sarbanes-Oxley:Will you need a forensic accountant?[J]. *Journal of Corporate Accounting and Finance*, 2005, 16(3): 69-75.

[14] Cohen, M., Crain, M. A. Sanders, A. Skills Used in Litigation Services[J]. *Journal of Accountancy*, 1996,v. 182, i. 3, p. 101.

[15] Copeland, J. D. *How to be an effective expert witness*[M]. Veterinary Clinics of North America: Small Animal Practice,1993, 23:1007-1017.

[16] Craig, R., & P. Reddy. Assessments of the expert evidence of accountants [J]. *Australian Accounting Review*, 2004, 14: 73-81.

[17] Crain, M., D. Goldwasser, & E. Harry. Expert witnesses-in jeopardy?[J]. *Journal of Accountancy*, 1994, December: 42-48.

[18] Crumbley, D., Heitger, L., & Smith, G. *Forensic and Investigative Accounting* (5th ed.)[M]. Chicago, IL, USA: CCH Inc,2011.

[19] DiGabriele, J. A.An Empirical Investigation of the Relevant Skills of Forensic Accountants[J]. *Journal of Education for Business*,2008, July/August:331-338.

[20] Feder, H.*Succeeding as an expert witness: Increasing your impact and income*[M]. New York, USA: Van Nostrand Reinhold, 1991.

[21] Harris, C. K., & Brown, A. M.The Qualities of Forensic Accountant[J]. *Pennsylvania CPA Journal*, 2000, 71 (1): 20.

[22] Harrison, J. Reconceptualizing the Expert Witness: Social Costs, Current Controls and Proposed Responses[J]. *Yale Journal on Regulation*,

2001,18(253): 1-46.

[23] Houck, M.M., M. Kranacher, B. Morris, R.A. Riley, J. Robertson, & J.T.Wells. Forensic Accounting as an Investigative Tool [J].*The CPA Journal*, 2006, 76(8): 68-70.

[24] Kothari, C. *Research Methodology, Methods & Techniques*[M]. New Delhi: New Age, 2006.

[25] Kumar, R. *Research Methodology - A step-by-step guide for beginners*[M]. London: Sage Publications, 2011.

[26] Manning, G.A. *Financial investigation and forensic accounting* [M]. Boca Raton: Taylor and Francis Group, 2005.

[27] Matson, J. V. *Effective expert witnessing* (3rd ed.) [M]. New York: CRC Press, 1999.

[28] McGaw, Renee. Forensic Accounting Gaining in Numbers [J].*Denver Business Journal*, 2006, August 25.

[29] Messmer, M. Exploring options in forensic accounting [J]. *National Public Accountant*,2004, 5: 9-20.

[30] Montgomery, R. H. *Auditing Theory and Practice*[M]. New York: Ronald Press, 1916

[31] Murphy, J. *Expert testimony : Maryland evidence handbook* (2nd ed.) [M]. Charlottesville, VA: Michie Company, 1993.

[32] Pagano, W. J., & Buckhoff, T. A. *Expert Witnessing in Forensic Accounting*[M]. United States: R.T. Edwards, 2005.

[33] Pallant, J. SPSS Survival Manual (2nd ed.)[M]. Maidenhead, UK: McGraw-Hill Education,2005.

[34] Peterson, B., & Reider, B. An examination of forensic accounting courses: Content and learning activities[J]. *Journal of Forensic Accounting*,2001, 2, 25-42.

[35] Ponemon, L. Auditor underreporting of time and moral reasoning: An experimental-lab study [J]. *Contemporary Accounting Research*, 1992b, Fall: 171-189.

[36] Ponemon, L. Ethical judgments in accounting: A cognitive-developmental perspective [J]. *Critical Perspectives on Accounting*, 1990, 1 (2): 191-215.

[37] Ponemon, L. Ethical reasoning and selection-socialization in accounting [J]. *Accounting, Organizations and Society*, 1992a, April/May: 239-258.

[38] Ponemon, L., & D. Gabhart. Auditor independence judgments: A cognitive developmental model and experimental evidence [J]. *Contemporary Accounting Research*, 1990, Fall: 227-251.

[39] Ponemon, L., & D. Gabhart. *Ethical Reasoning in Accounting and Auditing*. [M], Canada: Canadian General Accountants' Research Foundation, 1993.

[40] Ponemon, L., & D. Gabhart. Ethical reasoning research in the accounting and auditing professions.*In Moral Development in the Professions*, edited by J. Rest and D. Narvaez. Hillsdale[M], NJ: Lawrence Erlbaum Associates, 1994.

[41] Pope, K., & Ong, B. Strategies for Forming an Effective Forensic Accounting Team [J] , *The CPA Journal*, 2007, April 1.

[42] Poynter, D. *Expert witness handbook: Tips and techniques for the litigation consultant*[M]. Santa Barbara, CA: Para Publishing,1997.

[43] Previos, G. *The Scope of CPA Services: A Study of the Development of the Concepts of Independence and the Profess ion's Role in Society* [M]. New York, NY: Wiley, 1986.

[44] Quigley, F. M. Responsibilities of the consultant and expert witness[J]. *Focus on Critical Care*,1991,18: 238-239.

[45] Ramaswamy, V. Corporate governance and the forensic accountant[J]. *CPA Journal*, 2005,75, 68-70.

[46] Rasmussen, D. G., & Leauanae, J. L. Expert witness qualifications and selection[J]. *Journal of Financial Crime*, 2004, 12 (4), 165-171.

[47] Rechtman, Y. Forensic computing: A review of a growing technical field [J].*The CPA Journal*, 2006, 76(7): 68-69.

[48] Rix, K. J. B. The new Civil Procedure Rules. 1. The process of dispute resolution and litigation [J]. *Advances in Psychiatric Treatment*, 2000a, 6, 153-158.

[49] Saks, M. J., & Wissler, R. Legal and psychological bases of expert testimony: Surveys of the law and of jurors[J]. Behavioral Sciences & the Law,1984, 2, 435-449.

[50] Satyanarayan, T. Forensic Accounting and Corporate [J]. *The Chartered Accountant*, 2005:Vol. 53, No. 8.

[51] Scarrow, A. M. Providing expert witness testimony[J]. *Surgical Neurology*,2002, 57 (4), 278-282.

[52] Singleton, T. W., & Singleton, A. J. *Fraud Auditing and Forensic Accounting* (4th ed.)[M]. New York: Wiley,2010.

[53] Telpner, Z., & Mostek, M. S. *Expert Witnessing in Forensic Accounting: Handbook for Lawyers and Accounts*[M]. United States: CRC Press,2002.

[54] Wallace, A. The Role of the Forensic Accountant [J]. *Accountant*, November 1991.

[55] Weikel, W. J., & Hughes, P. The counselor as expert witness. ACA Legal series (Vol. 5). Alexandria, VA: American Counseling Association, 1993.

[56] Wells, J. The fraud examiners [J]. *Journal of Accountancy*, 2003, 196: 76.

[57] Wells, J. When you suspect fraud [J]. *Journal of Accountancy*, 2005, 199: 82-85.

[58] White, B. *Writing your MBA Dissertation*[D]. London: Thomson Learning, 2002.

[59] Wilkerson, A. P. Forensic psychiatry: The making and breaking of expert opinion testimony[J]. *The Journal of Psychiatry and Law*, 1997, Spring, 51-112.

[60] Woolf, E. *Legal Liabilities of Practicing Accountants* [M]. London: Butterworths and Co, 1984.

Appendix A　附录 A

Questionnaire　调查表

1. What is your profession ?　_____ .
· Forensic Accountant
· Expert Witness
· Civil or Criminal Attorney

1. 你的职业是什么?　_____ 。
· 法务会计
· 专家证人
· 民事或刑事律师

2. What is your level of education ? Please select whichever applies: _____ .
· Certified Education
· Master's Level
· Doctorate Level

2. 你的教育水平是什么样的? 请选择适用的选项 :_____ 。
· 认证教育
· 硕士
· 博士

3. How many years have you been practicing ?　_____ .
· 0–5 years
· 6–10 years
· 11–15 years
· More than 15 years

3. 你工作多少年了？ _____ 。

· 0 ~ 5 年

· 6 ~ 10 年

· 11 ~ 15 年

· 15 年以上

4. What should be area（s）of specialty that you believe are appropriate for a forensic accountant and expert witness？（You can choose more than 1 option）_____ .

· Forensic Expert

· Accountant Witness

· Bankruptcy, insolvency and reorganization

· Computer forensic analysis

· Economic damage calculations

· Family law

· Financial statement misrepresentations

· Fraud prevention, detection and response

· Valuation

4. 对于法务会计和专家证人，您认为哪些专业领域是合适的？（您可以选择多个选项）_____ 。

· 法务专家

· 会计证人

· 破产、无力偿债和重组

· 计算机法务分析

· 经济损失计算

· 家庭法

· 财务报表虚假陈述

· 预防、发现和应对欺诈

· 估价

Please answer next questions, using the rating scale provided （Strongly Agree, Agree, Neutral, Disagree, and Strongly Disagree）?

请用所提供的评分表回答下一个问题（强烈同意、同意、中立、不同意和强烈不同意）?

5. Essential skills needed for a forensic accountant_____ .

· Ability to identify frauds with minimal information

· Interviewing skills

· Knowledge of evidence

· Presentation of findings

· Knowledge of investigative techniques

· Investigative skills and mentality

· Identification of financial issues

· Interpretation of financial information

5. 法务会计必备的基本技能_____ 。

· 能够用最少的信息识别欺诈

· 面试技巧

· 证据知识

· 介绍调查结果

· 调查技术知识

· 调查技能和心态

· 确定财务问题

· 解读财务信息

6. Essential competencies needed for a forensic accountant_____ .

· Deductive analysis

· Critical thinking

· Unstructured problem solving

· Investigative flexibility

· Analytical proficiency

· Oral & written communication

· Specific legal knowledge

· Composure

6. 法务会计师必须具备的基本能力＿＿＿＿＿＿。

· 演绎分析

· 批判性思维

· 非结构化问题解决

· 调查灵活性

· 分析能力

· 口头和书面交流

· 特定法律知识

· 镇静

7. Essential traits and characteristics for a forensic accountant＿＿＿＿＿＿.

· Adaptive and team player

· Skepticism and inquisitive

· Analytical and evaluative

· Function well under pressure

· Generate new ideas and scenarios

· Detail oriented & Insightful

· Make people feel at ease

· Intuitive and Responsive

7. 法务会计的基本特征与特点＿＿＿＿＿＿。

· 适应性和团队精神

· 怀疑和好奇

· 分析和评估

· 在压力下运行良好

· 产生新的想法和场景

· 注重细节和洞察力

· 让人们感到放心

· 直观、反应灵敏

8. Essential skills and abilities needed for an expert witness_____ .

· Ability to persuade others

· Analytical ability

· Inquisitive skills

· Reasoning skills and abilities

· Mediagenic abilities

· Prior experience

· Public speaking ability

· Teaching and writing abilities

8. 专家证人所需的基本技能和能力_____ 。

· 说服他人的能力

· 分析能力

· 好奇技能

· 推理技能和能力

· 媒体能力

· 以往经验

· 演讲能力

· 教学和写作能力

9. Essential traits and characteristics for expert witness_____ .

· Knowledge, education, and training

· Experience

· Investigative orientation

· Ability to formulate an objective opinion

· Credibility

· Ability to provide consistent testimony

9. 专家证人的基本特征＿＿＿＿＿＿。

· 知识、教育和培训

· 经验

· 调查方向

· 能够提出客观意见

· 可信度

· 提供一致的证词的能力

10. Essential requirements for a forensic accountant to be an expert witness ＿＿＿＿＿ .

· Academic qualifications

· Professional training

· Extensive experience

· Excellent communication skills

· Teaching abilities

· Skeptic and diplomat

10. 法务会计作为鉴定人的基本要求＿＿＿＿＿＿。

· 学历

· 专业培训

· 丰富的经验

· 出色的沟通技巧

· 教学能力

· 有怀疑精神或相关文凭

11. Did you ever play the role of an expert witness in testimony in corporate business problems ? ＿＿＿＿＿ .

· Yes

· No

11.你曾经在公司业务问题上扮演过专家证人的角色吗？ ＿＿＿＿＿＿＿＿＿ 。

· 是

· 否

12. Do you think a forensic accountant can be an expert witness as well ?

＿＿＿＿＿＿＿＿＿ .

· Yes

· No

12. 你认为法务会计也可以做专家证人吗？ ＿＿＿＿＿＿＿＿＿ 。

· 是

· 否

Appendix B　附录 B

Component Matrix a 分量矩阵 a

	Component 成分							
	1	2	3	4	5	6	7	8
Essential skills FA – Knowledge of investigative techniques 法务会计的基本技能——调查技术知识	0.671			0.310				
Essential skills FA – Investigative skills and mentality 法务会计的基本技能——调查技能和心态	0.663							
Essential skills FA – Ability to identify frauds with minimal information 法务会计的基本技能——以最少的信息识别欺诈的能力	0.612						−0.470	
Essential skills FA – Presentation of findings 法务会计的基本技能——展示调查结果	0.591		0.395	0.355				
Essential skills FA – Interviewing Skills 法务会计的基本技能——面试技巧	0.530							

续表

Essential Competencies FA – Deductive analysis 法务会计的基本能力——演绎分析	−0.525		0.387	0.316			
Essential Competencies FA – Specific legal knowledge 法务会计的基本能力——特定法律知识	−0.515					−0.396	0.325
Essential Competencies FA – Critical Thinking 法务会计的基本能力——批判性思维	−0.467		0.392	0.323	0.353		
Essential Competencies FA – Oral and written communication 法务会计的基本能力——口头和书面沟通	−0.440	0.389					
Characteristics of FA – Analytical and evaluative 法务会计的特点——分析与评价		0.616		−0.309			
Essential Competencies FA –Analytical Proficiency 法务会计的基本能力——分析能力		0.611			−0.314		
Characteristics of FA – Adaptive and team player 法务会计的特点——适应与团队合作		0.603	−0.329				

续表

Essential Competencies FA –Unstructured Problem Solving 法务会计的基本能力——非结构化问题解决	−0.386	0.578				−0.334	
Characteristics of FA – Generate new ideas and scenarios 法务会计的特点——产生新的想法和场景		0.564			−0.387		
Characteristics of FA – Detail oriented and insightful 法务会计的特点——面向细节、富有洞察力			0.616	−0.313			
Characteristics of FA –Make people feel at ease 法务会计的特点——让人感到轻松			0.579				
Characteristics of FA – Function well under pressure 法务会计的特点——压力下的工作			−0.492			0.350	
Essential skills FA – Knowledge of Evidence 法务会计的基本技能——证据知识			0.365	0.350			−0.358

续表

Essential Competencies FA–Investigative flexibility 法务会计的基本能力——调查灵活性			0.644					
Characteristics of FA – Skepticism and inquisitive 法务会计的特点——怀疑论与探究	0.392		−0.459	0.400				−0.380
Essential skills FA – Interpretation of financial information 法务会计的基本技能——财务信息解读				0.557				
Essential Competencies FA – Composure 法务会计的基本能力——镇静				0.431	0.658			
Characteristics of FA – Intuitive and Responsive 法务会计的的特点——直观、灵敏				0.420			0.457	0.302
Essential skills FA – Identification of financial issues 法务会计的基本技能——识别财务问题	0.333							0.543

Extraction Method: Principal Component Analysis. 提取方法：主成分分析。

a. 8 components extracted.a . 提取 8 种成分。

	Component 成分					
	1	2	3	4	5	6
Essential Characteristics of EW – Ability to formulate an objective opinion 专家证人的本质特征——发表客观意见的能力	0.720		−0.395			
Essential Characteristics of EW – Experience 专家证人的本质特征——经验	0.645				−0.378	−0.319
Essential Characteristics of EW – Ability to provide consistent testimony 专家证人的基本特征——提供一致证词的能力	0.641					
Essential Characteristics of EW – Credibility 专家证人的本质特征——可信度	0.586	−0.380				0.334
Essential Skills of EW – Analytical ability 专家证人的基本技能——分析能力	0.515	−0.501				
Essential Skills of EW – Public speaking ability 专家证人的基本技能——演讲能力	0.432		0.424		0.316	
Essential Skills of EW – Prior experience 专家证人的基本技能——以往经验	0.357	−0.626		0.343		
Essential Characteristics of EW – Investigative orientation 专家证人的本质特征——调查取向	0.430	0.313	−0.592			
Essential Skills of EW – Ability to persuade others 专家证人的基本技能——说服他人的能力	0.469		0.527		0.348	
Essential Skills of EW – Teaching and writing abilities 专家证人的基本技能——教学与写作能力	0.334		0.318	−0.671		

续表

Essential Skills of EW –Mediagenic abilities 专家证人的基本技能——媒体能力		0.379		−0.510	0.422	
Essential Characteristics of EW – Knowledge, education and training 专家证人的本质特征——知识、教育和训练		0.438	0.337	0.509		0.396
Essential Skills of EW – Inquisitive skills 专家证人的基本技能——好奇技能		0.389			−0.703	
Essential Skills of EW – Reasoning skills and abilities 专家证人的基本技能——推理技能和能力	0.418					0.591

Extraction Method: Principal Component Analysis. 提取方法：主成分分析。

a. 6 components extracted. a . 提取 6 种成分。